MAY GOD BLESS YOU

Martha Pullen

THE
DAR MUSEUM

THE DAR MUSEUM

Martha Pullen's Favorite Places Series

The Martha Pullen Company

Publisher: Martha Pullen
Editorial Direction: Kathy McMakin
Editorial Contribution: Amelia Johanson
Publications Director: Leighann Lott
Graphic Design: Shannon Miller
Embroidery Art: Angela Pullen Atherton
Copy Editing: Karen Pyne, Kay Swanson

✦ ✦ ✦ ✦ ✦ ✦ ✦ ✦

The Martha Pullen Company
149 Old Big Cove Road
Brownsboro, Alabama 35741
www.marthapullen.com

The DAR Museum

Author and Curator of Costume and Textiles: Alden O'Brien
Museum Director and Chief Curator: Diane L. Dunkley
Curatorial Assistant: Virginia Vis
Photography: Mark Gulezian, QuickSilver Photographers

Hoffman Media, LLC.

President: Phyllis Hoffman
Vice President/Manufacturing: Greg Baugh
Digital Imaging Specialist: Clark Densmore

✦ ✦ ✦ ✦ ✦ ✦ ✦ ✦

Hoffman Media, LLC.
1900 International Park Drive, Suite 50
Birmingham, Alabama 35243

Copyright © 2009 The Martha Pullen Company, a subsidiary of Hoffman Media, LLC. All rights reserved. No part of this publication may be reproduced in any form or by any means, electronic, photocopy or otherwise without written permission from The Martha Pullen Company.

Printed in the United States of America

ISBN: 978-1-878048-56-1

DAR MUSEUM

CONTENTS

Federal Era "Seamless" Baby Gown 14	Purple Velvet Spencer Jacket 76
Empire Waist Infant Gown...................... 16	Catherine Burroughs's Puffed Hem Dress 78
Back-Fastening Child's Frock 18	Lady's Unfinished Net Collar 82
Mary Ann Nickerson's Christening Dress 20	Chemisette 84
Charlotte Knox's Baptismal Dress 22	Nursing Gown 86
Cornucopia and Curlicue Ayrshire Dress 24	Embroidered Corset 88
Fifty-One Pleats Baby Dress 28	Blue and Brown Dressing Coat
Pleated Yoke with Smocked Bodice 30	with White Tiered Petticoat 90
Pintucks and Lace Christening Gown 32	Anna Holyoke's Wedding Dress 92
Ayrshire Work Toddler Dress 36	Dressing Sacque and Bustle Petticoat 94
John Briggs's Blue Skeleton Suit 38	Mary Emma Funk's Wedding Dress 96
Gathered Bodice Summer Dress 40	Young Lady's Shirred Dressing Gown 98
Broderie Anglaise Girl's Dress 42	Alma Brooks's Wedding Dress 100
Eva May Ratcliffe's Drop-waist Dress 44	Redwork Embroidered Combing Jacket 102
Linen Boy's Jacket 46	Aesthetic Style Wisteria Tea Gown 104
Harvey Glidden's Red Dress 48	Creamy Satin Wedding Gown 108
Raglan Sleeve Muslin Dress 50	Gauze Over Silk Edwardian Gown 112
Appliquéd Floral Embroidered Dress 52	Lingerie Style Graduation Dress 116
Late Victorian Girl's Dress 54	Henrietta Malone's Dainty Nightgown 118
Princess Panel Toddler's Dress 56	Sarah Radcliffe's Wedding Dress 120
Pink Cotton Smocked Dress 58	Jean Mackay's Wedding Dress 122
Faux Needlepoint Wool Dress 60	Ivory Satin Wedding Waistcoat 124
Young Boy's Skeleton Suit 62	Embroidered Cotton Sleeved Waistcoat 126
Checked Weave Everyday Pinafore 64	Rococo Swags Cutaway Waistcoat 128
Ice-Blue Satin Quilted Petticoat 66	Inaugural Ball Taffeta Waistcoat 130
Embroidered Transparent Muslin Gown 68	Thomas Rumrill's Wedding Waistcoat 132
Center Panel Embroidery Mull Gown 70	Young Boy's Satin Waistcoat 134
Neoclassical Mull Drawstring Gown 72	Cherry Red Winter Waistcoat 136
Ruched Bodice Evening Gown 74	Figured Silk Altered Waistcoat 138

DAR MUSEUM

DEDICATION

This book is dedicated with deep appreciation to the countless members of the National Society Daughters of the American Revolution – women who have been the keepers of family histories, stories and heirlooms and have entrusted these to the DAR Museum. By saving treasured baby clothes and other beautifully embellished garments, they have preserved pieces of early American history. By recording the history of these heirlooms, they have documented the history of early American women and children. By contributing family stories and heirlooms to provide for the education of future generations, they have created a legacy for our organization and our nation.

ACKNOWLEDGEMENTS

We acknowledge with gratitude the assistance of many people whose talents merged in the creation of this book. Mark Gulezian has been our unflappable photographer for years, and Jennifer White assisted him both during the photo shoot to prepare the clothing and afterwards during the photo editing process. Virginia Vis, quilt expert and textile conservator, cleaned many of the white cotton baby and ladies' dresses so they could look their best; she also catalogued in detail many of the garments so their descriptions could be complete and accurate. Mary Denise Smith helped dress manikins ahead of time, a task requiring both historic knowledge and skill; she also served as a quick-change artist during the photography. Both helped with edits and suggestions for the earliest drafts of the text, as did Louisa Eifrig Pineault long-distance from Minnesota. Megan Leonard, then a graduate student with the Corcoran College of Art and Design History of Decorative Arts Masters Program, took on an internship early in the process, organizing all 50-some garments slated for the book, tracking their locations, and determining which manikins they fit on, as well as coordinating washing and steaming. We also extend thanks to Megan's fellow graduate students, Leslie Nottingham and Kirsten Edwards, whom Megan recruited to help on the days of the photo shoot. They proved to be dab hands at the quick rotation of baby, toddler and ladies' manikins. The museum Registrars, Anne Ruta and Stephanie Randall, were invaluable with help and patience during the months of upheaval in which so many items of antique clothing were constantly moving between storage, conservator, workroom and manikins: keeping track of everything and finally making sure everything was back in its proper place.

The DAR Museum is fortunate to have the guidance of Michelle Mott Juehring, Curator General, whose interest in women's history and historic fashion have made her a particular pleasure to work with during the Calvin Administration.

We are indebted to Martha Pullen, a Distinguished Daughter, for her dedication to documenting and reviving the needle arts presented in this book, and her outstanding support and promotion of the DAR Museum.

We are grateful to Linda Gist Calvin, President General, NSDAR and the Calvin Administration who have provided enthusiastic support for this project.

LINDA GIST CALVIN
President General, NSDAR

THE DAR MUSEUM

Just two blocks from The White House stands Memorial Continental Hall, a magnificent marble building in the Beaux-Arts tradition, built between 1902 and 1910 by the National Society Daughters of the American Revolution as their headquarters. Originally meant to serve as offices, auditorium and a fire-proof repository for "papers and relics," the Hall now contains one of the nation's premier genealogical libraries, surrounded by period rooms, which are part of the DAR Museum.

The National Society Daughters of the American Revolution was founded in 1890. Galvanized by being denied membership in the Sons of the American Revolution, founded in 1889, a group of American women decided to start their own organization, honoring their ancestors, both men and women, who had supported the cause of liberty during the Revolutionary War. As a requirement for membership, a woman must prove her descent from someone (man or woman) who aided the American side either by fighting, feeding the troops, supplying goods or money or serving in the new United States Government. Every DAR member since the beginning has filled out the charts and records to prove her lineage.

Since the Centennial of the Declaration of Independence in 1876, Americans have exhibited a renewed appreciation for their history and the objects of their country's past. Many historical and genealogical societies were founded in the years between 1876 and 1900. The DAR has emerged as one of the most successful and long-lived of those societies. The newly founded society chose as its goals Historic Preservation, Education and Patriotism. From the beginning, the Daughters wanted to preserve the objects of the past, and "to study the manners and measures of those days. Especially, it is desired to preserve some record of the heroic deeds of American

DAR MUSEUM

women." Almost immediately the society began to collect items used by the ancestors of its members. Over the years, the relics and handicrafts of women filled the DAR collection. Quilts, coverlets, samplers, clothing and other like items found a home in DAR headquarters long before most other museums began to recognize their value. More than 100 years later, the DAR Museum continues to preserve the objects and exhibit them in two galleries and 31 period rooms and record the deeds of American women and men.

The DAR Museum costume collection encompasses at least 200 years of American history, as shown through the clothing, jewelry and accessories of our ancestors. Baby caps and dresses, wedding gowns, everyday and fancy dress as well as mourning clothing and jewelry represent the lives of their makers and previous owners. DAR members have donated the majority of the collection; their family histories add historical interest and sometimes poignant stories to the garments themselves. The museum's costume exhibitions, in the museum's main galleries, offer the visitor a chance to see these items up-close. Costume items are also often included in other types of exhibitions, so there is usually something costume-related to see at the DAR Museum.

Memorial Continental Hall is connected to DAR Constitution Hall, Washington DC's largest auditorium (by the Administration Building) and home to the DAR Museum gallery and shop. The entrance to DAR headquarters is at a most appropriate address: 1776 D Street, Northwest, Washington DC.

The DAR Museum is open Monday through Friday, 9:30 a.m. to 4 p.m. and on Saturdays, 9 a.m. to 5 p.m. The museum is closed on Sundays, national holidays and for the Daughters of the American Revolution annual meeting (about one week) every year. For information about the DAR Museum, call 202-879-3241 or check the website at www.dar.org/museum.

DIANE L. DUNKLEY
Museum Director and Chief Curator

CONTRIBUTORS

ALDEN O'BRIEN
Author
Curator of Costume and Textiles, DAR Museum

My love of historic costume seems to come from a combination of interests. Growing up in Chicago, I was taken to the Art Institute by my mother, and learned to love art—especially portraits with gorgeous clothes. I pored over my mother's and grandmother's childhood books with their illustrations of periods past. And I loved acting. I knew I wanted to be either a curator or an actress by the time I was 10, but didn't figure out how to blend my interest in costume and history until college. While an art history major at Barnard College, I was fortunate enough to serve as an intern in the costume collections at the Museum of the City of New York and the Smithsonian Institution. The Fashion Institute of Technology created a master's program in Museum Studies in Costume and Textiles just about the time I graduated from college. After completing my studies there, I spent a year as an assistant to the conservator of the First Ladies' Gowns. I've been at the DAR Museum since 1990, and have loved working with the small but exquisite collection of costume dating from the late 1700s to the early 1900s.

You'll notice that I haven't mentioned sewing…I am scarcely a step above novice, and most of my sewing has been for my daughters' Halloween costumes and school plays (you'll never see a more period-correct 1420s Cinderella!) I look at the exquisite details on garments such as those you'll see here with awe, knowing I will never achieve the level of skill needed to create them…although with the embroidery patterns made from them, perhaps I will dare to recreate them in part.

DIANE L. DUNKLEY
Museum Director and Chief Curator, DAR Museum

Diane Dunkley has been Museum Director and Chief Curator at the DAR Museum since 1990. At the headquarters of the Daughters of the American Revolution, she has coordinated several exhibits, including "Souvenirs from the Voyage of Life;" "Magnificent Intentions: Decorative Arts of the District of Columbia;" "George Washington: The Man Behind the Image; Bound for the West: Women and their Families on the Oregon Trail;" and "Martha Washington as an Icon of the Colonial Revival." She was co-curator of "True Love and a Happy Home: Cultural Expectations and Feminine Experiences in Victorian America," and "Talking Radicalism in a Greenhouse: Women Writers and Women's Rights." She was the lead curator of the ground-breaking exhibition "Forgotten Patriots: African American and American Indian Service in the American Revolution." Her current exhibition projects include a major loan exhibition celebrating 250 years of Wedgwood.

Prior to coming to the DAR, Ms. Dunkley was with the Colonial Williamsburg Foundation for 10 years, serving as Manager of the Governor's Palace and as Curator of Carter's Grove, a James River plantation house. She has written articles about Carter's Grove and the Colonial Revival for Colonial Williamsburg, and for The Interpreter, both publications of the Colonial Williamsburg Foundation.

She is a graduate of East Carolina University, and holds a master's degree in history from the College of William and Mary. As a student at William and Mary, she worked in costume as a historic interpreter at Colonial Williamsburg. Although as a senior in high school she was a Betty Crocker Homemaker of Tomorrow, she reluctantly admits that she no longer is able to find time to practice the art of the needle.

MARK GULEZIAN
Photographer

Mark Gulezian began QuickSilver Photographers in 1981 in Washington, D.C. to provide professional-quality photography to artists, museums and institutions. His photography of artwork and museum objects has appeared in books and other publications worldwide.

VIRGINIA VIS
Curatorial Assistant, DAR Museum

After 14 years as Wardrobe Supervisor for the Arena Stage in Washington D.C., Virginia Vis began her own business cleaning and repairing quilts and other textiles in 1994. In addition to being Project Manager for the Quilt Index at the DAR museum in 2006, she has been a volunteer in the museum's quilt collection since 2002. While working with Curator Alden O'Brien, she compiled the Museum's educational slide program titled "Masterpieces of the DAR Quilt Collection" and assisted with the "Quilts of a Young Country" loan exhibit at The International Quilt Festival in Houston, Texas in the fall of 2008.

Federal Era "Seamless" BABY GOWN

Turn of the 19th Century

"The little child was gone to rest in its cradle, where clean linen added refreshment to its peaceful slumbers."
–"MORAL TALE: THE NOTABLE DAUGHTER," *The Children's Magazine: Calculated for the Use of Families and Schools,* March 1798

The mystery to the modern eye examining this dream of a baby dress is where on earth are the side seams? None is visible, until a very careful study underneath the embroidery on the right side reveals two 1/2-inch lengths of seam allowance in between the vertical and horizontal embroidery. The mystery is solved: The clever needlewoman covered her seam with the heavier white cotton embroidery thread, and worked her eyelets right over them! Only the embroidery now connects front and back panels.

The soft, sheer cotton, called "mull," used for this little dress was imported from India. It is the same cotton used for fashionable women's dresses in the late 1790s and early 1800s. Unlike women's dresses, such as the two early 19th century mulls in this book, which were pre-embroidered in India, this one must have been embroidered after construction, given the embroidery over the seam.

Instead of a high-waist silhouette echoing that of Mama's dress, this federal-era (1785 to 1815) baby's dress has no waistline in front. Framing the front of the skirt is an inverted V arrangement of whitework and large eyelet embroidery, which is repeated straight down the sides of the dress, with a large central motif below the center-front neckline. The hem is embroidered with an intricate scalloped floral eyelet design with a simple needle-lace grid filling the center of each flower.

A 1/4-inch wide shoulder piece embroidered with padded satin-stitch dots connects the front and back of the dress. The back of the dress, behind the embroidery at the sides, has a drawstring casing made of the same mull at waist level and a casing at either side of the center back opening to fasten the neckline. Short, puffed sleeves are bound at the lower edge with a 1/4-inch self-band.

6935 Gift of Emeline A. Street

Empire Waist INFANT GOWN

1810

"We have a child on our knee, and a child on our table — our attention is occasionally diverted. There is something in the left hand and a something in the right — we kiss the one and scratch the other, and hardly know which should claim our more immediate attention."

—"FEELING," Something Ed. By Nemo Nobody, esq, March 17, 1810

This gown with its elaborate embroidery on sturdy white cotton was worn by a boy named J. Hamilton Shapley, born in 1810 in New Hampshire. It could also, of course, have been worn by his sisters and brothers; but its use by a boy reminds us that 18th and 19th century parents did not believe babies needed to proclaim gender in their dress.

The high waist, low neck and narrow skirts of ladies' fashions of the time period are reflected in the tiny bodice, a mere 1-1/2-inches deep at center front, and in the skirt, which is scarcely gathered and flares just slightly towards the hem. Also like contemporaneous women's dresses, two drawstrings at the neck, one in front and one in back, and a third at the waist, hold the dress together in back. Like children's clothes of the day, it is open down the back; and with Yankee practicality seemingly at odds with the elaborate embroidery, the center back edge is an unhemmed selvedge. Early 19th century baby gowns are not as long as later ones, and this one measures 31-inches from waist to hem in front.

Extremely short sleeves have a triangular, folded-back cuff made in a separate piece. The neck and sleeves are edged in buttonhole-stitched loops resembling tatting.

The cynosure of the dress is ornate embroidery in two rows with ribbon-like scrolls down the front of the skirt, which are alternately filled with French knots, bullion stitch and padded satin stitch. Between the scrolls are flowers with eyelet centers, the petals worked in buttonhole stitch so as to raise the edges slightly above the fabric, giving the flowers a somewhat three-dimensional quality. Inside these vertical borders are little flower-bud sprigs. Another pattern of scrolls wends around the hem, alternating French knots and bullion fillings.

2469 Gift of Mrs. Robert Allen Reid

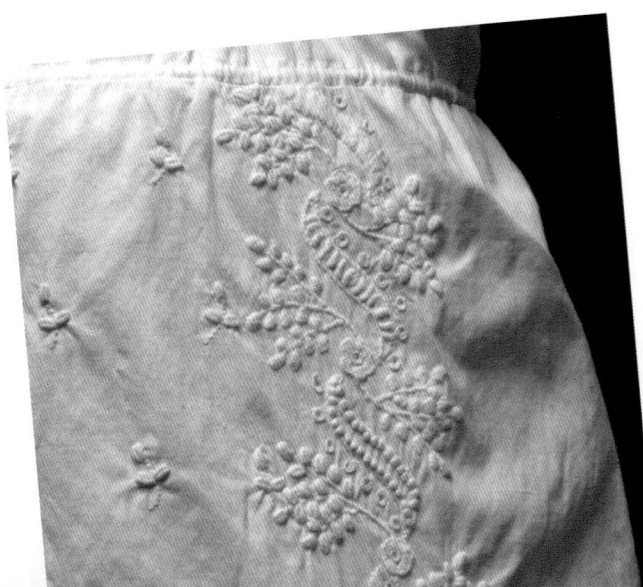

"Sweet babe! thou'st just begun to be,
To toss on life's tumultuous sea;
Those eyes have just received their hue
Of fluid and cerulean blue;
Thy little cheek but youngly glows
With all the blushing of the rose;
How feeble is that frame of thine,
My lovely infant Josephine."

–EXCERPT "TO MY INFANT DAUGHTER,"
The Philadelphia Repertory, September 8, 1810

DAR MUSEUM

Back-Fastening CHILD'S FROCK

About 1810

This baby's dress of about 1810 shows not only how children's and even babies' clothes imitated ladies' styles of their day, but how in the early 19th century, the borrowing went both ways—children's back-fastening frocks (in French, "robe a l'enfant," or child's-style dress) were adopted into women's fashions. The back fastening of the frock had been traditional construction for children for centuries. It was only about 1800 that women's dresses began to open in back.

This frock fastens with drawstrings at the back; double drawstrings are found at both neckline and waistline. The upper drawstring at the waist extends from center back only as far as the beginning of the triangular panel at the front. Like most babies' and young children's frocks, the back is open all down the center back, and would have revealed a slip underneath.

French knots and tiny, pinhead-size eyelets make up most of the decoration. The high-waisted bodice is gently gathered, with a triangular panel at the waist; the base is the front waistline, and the point rises in a gentle curve towards center front. This triangle is echoed on the sleeves. Each triangle is outlined with a row of tiny eyelets framed by double rows of French knots. Inside the bodice panel are two interlocking circles of eyelets inside French-knot circles, with a small satin-stitch leafy sprig inside, and larger ones outside each circle. The sleeves are slightly shirred to match the bodice, and their triangular panels are embroidered in backstitched vines, berries made with French knots and satin-stitch leaves.

The sleeves, skirt hem and center back opening have a decorative scalloped edge; the hem's slightly larger in scale, finished in buttonhole stitch and a continuous row of eyelets outlining the scallops. Above the hem, a series of ribbon-like scroll shapes and satin-stitch leafy sprigs wend gracefully around the bottom edge, with French knots outlining the scrolls, and eyelets inside them; between the scrolls are French knot circles around eyelet flowers. The bodice is only 3-inches high, and the overall length is 32-inches at center back. The hem circumference is 33-inches—narrow compared to later babies' gowns, and another reflection of the silhouette in fashion at the time.

4084.1 Gift of Bernice Webb Putnam

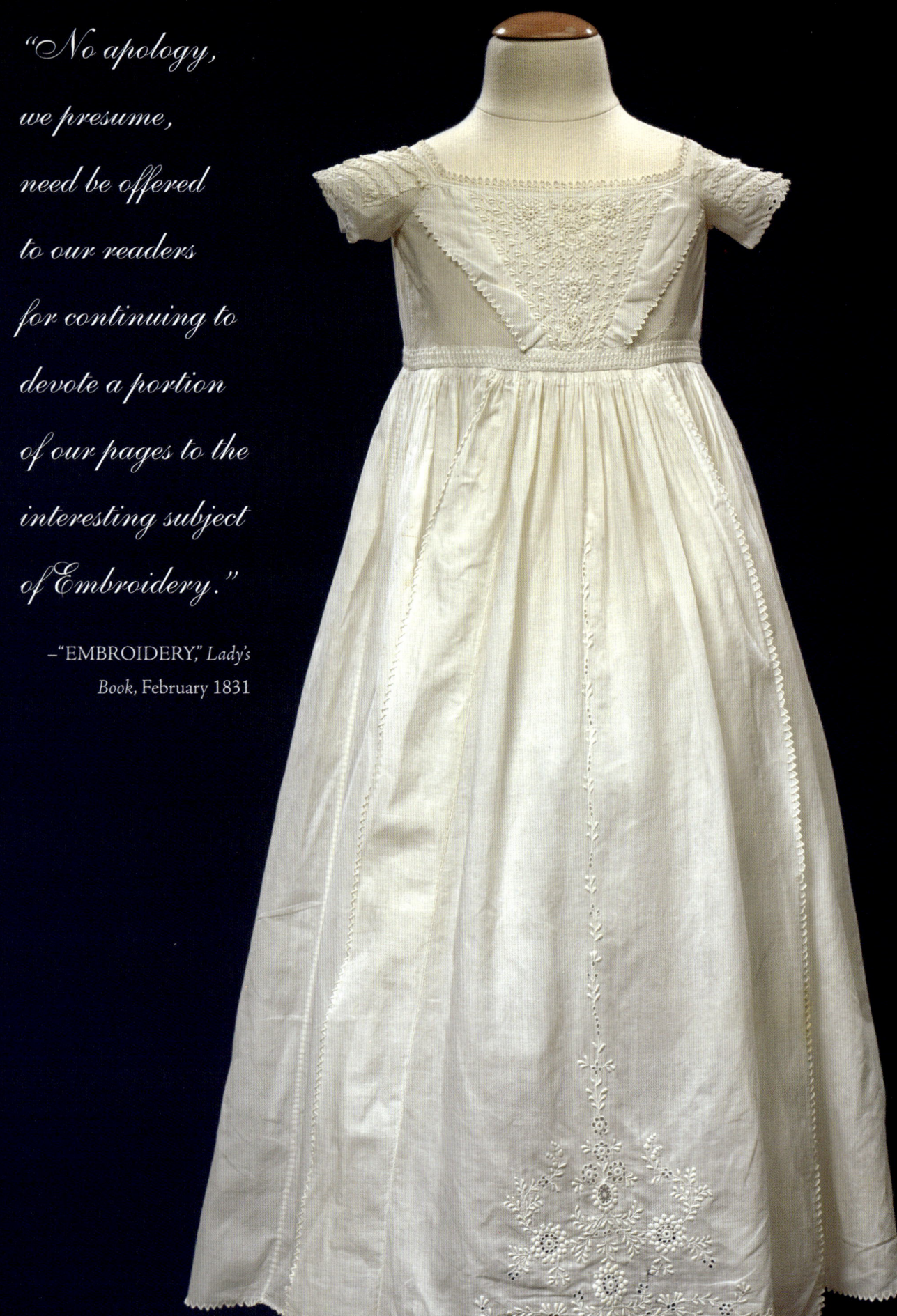

"No apology, we presume, need be offered to our readers for continuing to devote a portion of our pages to the interesting subject of Embroidery."

—"EMBROIDERY," *Lady's Book*, February 1831

Mary Ann Nickerson's CHRISTENING DRESS

1831

This lovely little Ayrshire dress is said to be Mary Ann Nickerson's christening dress worn in Chatham on Cape Cod in Massachusetts in 1831. The Ayrshire infant gowns were introduced in the 1820s, and the 1830s would have been the height of their popularity. The slightly raised waist would fit this date. Even though babies' bodies lack a defined waist, clothes for infants echoed women's styles in the placement of the waistlines.

The bodice and bottom of the skirt are embroidered with matching stylized flowers, some with two rows of "petals" surrounding the needle-lace-filled openwork, and other flowers slightly simpler with openwork petals. Two rows of leafy sprigs march along the edges of the bodice center panel. At the hem, the flowers are surrounded with additional floral and foliate sprays, and a single row of leaves and eyelets wends its way up towards the waist. Overall, the hem's main area of decoration is only 5-inches high. This would have allowed Mary Ann's mother to convert the baby dress into a toddler's by using only the embroidered lower part of the skirt, had she desired to do so. A skirt with more elaborate embroidery in the upper area would be too much of a shame to cut down! The skirt is made in two pieces, seamed at the sides, and is gauged into a waistband, which features an abstract leaf design embroidered in satin stitch.

The edges of the bodice, the skirt flanges and the skirt hem have pointed scalloped edging finished in buttonhole stitch. The neckline trim has an eyelet in each scallop. These pointed scallops were common in whitework embroidery done for women's accessories of the 1820s and 1830s such as the elaborate pelerine collars; they were called "Vandyke" edgings, or simply "vandyking," after the pointed lace edgings seen in Anthony Van Dyck's 17th century portraits of English royalty and nobility. The neckline has a similar vandyked scallop with single eyelets in each scallop.

The raglan sleeves have three rows of self-fabric trim with eyelets above scalloped-edged (rounded, not vandyked) trim, applied on the top side of the sleeve only, beneath embroidery at the shoulder. The lowest of the three rows of trim has satin-stitch, teardrop-shaped motifs above the eyelets. The sleeves end with an eyelet and scalloped edge with satin-stitched leafy sprigs. The dress has no visible method of fastening at center back, but the two-layer waistband may have served as a casing for a ribbon. The back of the neckline has a drawstring casing, but no surviving tape or cord.

62.131 Gift of Irmah W. Kerrigan

"I am thinking, my dear, of two events when I shall be the happiest of my life."

"And pray, what may they be, Dr.?" remarked the lady.

"One is the hour when I shall call you my wife, for the first time."

"And the other?"

"It is when we shall present our first-born for baptism."

"What, sprinkled!"

"Yes, my dear, sprinkled."

"Never shall a child of mine be sprinkled!"

"Every child of mine shall be sprinkled."

"They shall be, hey!"

"Yes, my love."

"Well sir, I can tell you then, that your babies won't be my babies. So, good night, sir."

The lady left the room, and the doctor left the house. The sequel to this true story was, that the Dr. never married, and the lady is an old maid.

–"OLLA PODRIDA,"
Spirit of the Times, March 1852

DAR MUSEUM

Charlotte Knox's BAPTISMAL DRESS

1852

Delicate, intricate Ayrshire embroidery, which combines whitework and eyelets with needle-lace fillings, is used to beautiful effect in this dress worn at Charlotte Knox's baptism in 1852. Family history relates that it was already "old" at that time, which is entirely possible, as Ayrshire work began in the late 1810s and would die out a mere decade after Charlotte was baptized. The design of the embroidery uses an abundance of intricate needle-lace-filled eyelets, giving the embroidery an especially airy quality.

The bodice, which is lined with white cotton in front only, has a wide, moderately low neckline typical of the first half of the 19th century. The neckline has a drawstring casing with a decorative scalloped and eyelet-embroidered edge. A truncated center V panel in the bodice is bordered by flanges characteristic of Ayrshire infant dresses, being edged with a scalloped cutwork and embroidered design. The Ayrshire panel has a central five-petal flower – the petals, center, and surrounding leaves filled with elaborate needle-lace. Around the central flower, satin-stitch leafy sprigs fill the areas around the openwork areas. The panel is bordered with a row of tiny needle-lace-filled flowers and an outer row of stylized openwork flowers with satin-stitch leaves surrounding them, resembling paisley designs.

The waistband is plain white cotton under a band of embroidery, in which diagonal rows of simple eyelets alternate with two five-leaved sprigs of whitework. The 81-inch circumference skirt is gathered into the waistband, with more Ayrshire embroidery in the center panel, and a row of drawn work immediately inside the flanges, which match that of the bodice. The neckline in the back is also trimmed with a falling collar that reflects the shape of the flanges. The flanges and the entire hem of the skirt are edged with matching scalloped, eyelet edges.

The short sleeves are elaborately constructed and decorated. They are extensively embroidered at the top, and have three overlapping cuffs facing upwards, each edged with eyelet scallops, the outermost cuff having more floral embroidery. Finally, the sleeve ends with a plain band of cotton with a scalloped edge.

A drawstring in the neck fastens in back, but no fastening is visible at the waist. Since the waistband has two layers, it may have had a ribbon threaded through it to tie at the waist.

Measured from center front, the bodice is 4-inches high, the waistband is 1-inch wide and the skirt is 38-1/2-inches long.

2848.2 Gift of Mrs. Franklin R. Grundrum

"An infant's outfit just completed at a popular furnishing house has a dozen of each of the most essential garments. The dresses are French nansook, trimmed with tucks, puffs, and ruffles and a little lace. Neatly "done up" and folded in boxes a wagon was required to carry them home. The price was $375. The christening robe at $75, was not included in the bill."

—"NEW YORK FASHIONS,"
Harper's Bazaar, October 1886

Cornucopia and Curlicue
AYRSHIRE DRESS

Pre-1864

Ayrshire embroidery at its most breathtaking makes this dress stand out from the hundred baby dresses in the museum's collection. Typical mid-century Ayrshire style is seen here in the rounded neckline and V-shaped bodice panel thick with eyelets and embroidery flanked by wing-like flanges or robings embroidered to coordinate. The skirt is decorated "en tablier" (French for "apron-style"), in a reverse V defined by more embroidered robings, framing embroidery, which widens towards the hem. At least five Eichelberger children were christened in this dress between 1864 and 1872. Since the Ayrshire embroidery industry had essentially died out by the mid-1860s, partly due to Britain's inability to acquire American-made cotton during our Civil War, the dress was probably already an heirloom when someone began keeping track in 1864, but no earlier history is known.

DAR MUSEUM

Central to the bodice panel, a slightly truncated V shape typical of Ayrshire gowns, are two flowers with eyelet centers and needle-lace filled leaves. Above these float many tiny flowers with needle-lace petals or centers. The remainder of the panel is filled with a host of abstract curlicues in needle-lace eyelets, curling every which way, which give an energy to the design. The bodice robings are bordered with a restrained repeat of dainty needle-lace petal flower with satin-stitch leaves, alternating with a single curlicue. The robings have scalloped edges, small satin-stitch circles in each scallop and a quatrefoil flower above each series of four scallops.

Somewhat atypically, a very narrow waistband separates bodice from skirt; it is decorated with two rows of white running stitch. The skirt is gauged in miniscule pleats into this waistband. The embroidery on the front panel of the skirt begins 2-1/2-inches below the waistband with tiny trails of fernlike leaves and flowers, which gradually widen and blend into the main, triangular embroidered area above the hem. Here, three stylized cornucopias, two at the hem and one at the pinnacle of the triangle, burst forth with a profusion of flowers and needle-lace leaves matching the work on the bodice. These are surrounded with still more flowers, leaves and curlicues.

The hem is a complicated scalloped edge with tiny embroidered quatrefoil flowers and rays of satin-stitch dots. This extends around the entire dress. The skirt robings curve gently at the hem and towards the bottom and are embroidered with floral and foliate sprays. The robings are edged throughout with eyelet scallops, and this edging continues around the entire hem of the skirt.

The sleeves have alternating, diagonally set panels of puffing with Swiss-embroidered insertions. The puffing is sewn not edge to edge with the insertion, but 1/8-inch inside the edge, so that the eyelet edges of the insertions form a little free-floating ruffle. The sleeves are edged with a narrow embroidered trim. The back is fastened with two small white shell buttons, now mismatched.

86.139.1 Gift of Mrs. Franklin R. Grundrum

"*Bear in mind what I am telling you, and that the hem and tucks are to be ironed very smoothly, always crosswise.*"

—"THE SEWING GIRL," *The American Monthly*, January 1865

DAR MUSEUM

Fifty-One Pleats BABY DRESS

Mid-19th Century

This dress is deceptively simple: relatively little embroidery belies the enormous amount of time it would have taken to make the skirt's fifty-one 1/8-inch tucks. The bodice, unlike the Ayrshire styles of approximately the same time frame, is relatively simple, decorated only in front with alternating vertical rows of Swiss embroidery and bobbin lace. The same embroidered band, backed with cotton, creates the waistband. A 66-inch circumference skirt is gauged to the waistband, ending with that extraordinary pleating above a scalloped edge with abstract embroidered floral motifs enclosed in an undulating wave.

The short sleeves are constructed of a combination of the three types of embellishment in the bodice and skirt: a band of the embroidery repeating that of the bodice, a band of bobbin lace, and a band of embroidered edging from the hem. The neck is edged with loops of what look like tatting, but on closer examination appear to be buttonhole stitch. The dress opens at back with a Dorset-style button at the neck and two more at the waist, all with 1/16-inch wide woven cotton tape loops. Like most baby dresses, this one has large side seams in the bodice to allow some expansion as the baby grew. This gown was worn by a member or members of the Hyatt family of Westchester County, New York.

87.42.1 Mrs. J. Frederick Pomeroy, Jr.

"The fullness is disposed in box-plaits into a yoke, either low or high-necked, as may be preferred. The high necked, long sleeved dresses are now generally preferred for babies' dresses in this climate."

—"EVERY-DAY DRESSES, GARMENTS, ETC.,"
Peterson's Magazine,
October 1873

DAR MUSEUM

Pleated Yoke
WITH SMOCKED BODICE

1870s

Not all beautifully made white baby dresses of the Victorian era are christening dresses: nearly all babies wore long white dresses, plain or elaborate depending on the parents' means. The length protected them from dreaded drafts for the first six months or so, after which they were put into "short clothes," or knee-length dresses, which would supposedly allow more freedom of movement for the "creeping" (crawling) and walking child. This dress could easily have been a regular, though elaborate, day dress for a child of the 1870s.

This batiste dress shows the influence of the Aesthetic Movement, which initiated the use of smocking in fashionable dress. Smocking, before about 1870, was only seen in rural laborers' smocks, not exclusively in England. Introducing it into fashionable English clothing not only showed an appreciation for the beauty of the technique, but was a semi-political statement. In line with the Aesthetes' return to handcrafted textiles, books and furniture, using smocking declared a rejection of machine-made embellishment in favor of handwork, and a respect for the rural laborer in the face of increasing industrialization.

The high-necked, sloping-shouldered yoke, with 1/4-inch vertical pleats, is made of one piece, and is rather haphazardly whip-stitched inside a square-necked bodice, the self-bound neckline decorated with featherstitching. Below this neckline, which can be cinched with a drawstring, a full bodice is gathered just above the waistband into three rows of smocking. A machine-made Valencienne lace ruffle edges the yoke, and a wider ruffle of Valenciennes decorates the neck.

The French seamed sleeves, made in one piece, are headed with a band of embroidered linen, with graceful flowers, buds and leaves wending their way between two rows of drawn work, above a row of featherstitching and a lace-edged ruffle made of 3/16-inch box pleats like those at the hem. The sleeve's cuffs are pleated to match the yoke with a ruffle of the wider Valencienne ruffle above it, and a ruffle of the same at the wrist.

With exquisite care, 93 inches of fabric have been gauged, with a breathtaking 40 pleats to the inch, into a 3/4-inch waistband; featherstitching covers the seam between bodice and waistband. The hem is decorated with seven 1/8-inch tucks above a band of embroidery matching the sleeve caps, and finally a 1-inch box-pleated, lace-edged ruffle. The overall length of the bodice is 6-inches, and the skirt is 33-inches, measured at the center front from neckline to hem.

7087 Gift of M.W. Livermore

"Imported christening robes are made of linen cambric, ornamented with the daintiest needle-work wrought on the garment, and the finest Valenciennes. Less expensive robes are of French nansook, soft, fine and of yellow-whiteness, like Indian muslin. The yoke and the broad tablier are formed of lengthwise bands of Valenciennes between puffs of nansook. The skirt may be finished by a deep hem headed by insertion, or else a flounce finished with lace."

–"NEW YORK FASHIONS: INFANTS' CLOTHING,"
Harper's Bazaar, June, 21 1873

Pintucks and Lace
CHRISTENING GOWN

About 1880

This exquisite batiste baby dress was worn by 10 children of Annie Maria Robinson Saunders, the owner of the shirred dressing gown elsewhere in this book, as well as several members of later generations, including the donors. Its center princess-style panel displays a myriad of net insertions and pintucks arranged in a symphony of pieced panels, edged with a hand-embroidered Valenciennes ruffle. A matching lace ruffle decorates the neck. The center panel extends from shoulder to shoulder, nips in slightly at what would be baby's waist level, if indeed babies had a defined waistline, with vertical tucks or darts; it widens to 22-inches at the hem.

Each area of decoration in the center panel is framed horizontally by a row of net lace insertion. From neck to about baby's knee or ankle level (11-inches), seven tiny vertical pintucks, with a small vertical dart near "waist" level, frame a central net lace insertion. At the shoulder and below the "waist," where the panel is wider than the pintucked area, are more vertical insertions.

Below this area is a series of bands with one, then two, then three mitred square net lace medallions on point, framed by pintucks and more insertions. The band with the single medallion has seven vertical pintucks on either side of the medallion and lace insertions between the tucks and the edge of the panel. A wide band separates the first and second bands of medallions; two repeats of eight horizontal pintucks are worked above a row of net lace insertion.

Vertical pintucks are found inside all the medallions, and a row of Valencienne insertion and a row of narrow net lace frames their bottom halves. But each medallion treats the area above it differently. The single medallion is framed identically with lace on all four sides. The double medallions have vertical tucks matching the ones inside them; the triple medallions have diagonal tucks.

Intriguingly, all the diagonal pintucks run in the same direction, from upper left to lower right, except for two areas at the extreme proper right in the lowest row, which run from lower left to upper right. Below the last band of medallions is a row of the embroidered net lace alongside two rows of the Valenciennes that frame the collar, sleeves and center panel. This lace continues around the entire hem, as does the pattern of medallions and pintucks from the lowest row in the panel. Above the medallions are two sets of six pintucks with a lace insertion below each set.

The full-length sleeves are decorated from above elbow level with a row of narrow insertion followed by vertical pintucks and insertions on the upper part of the sleeve only (the underside closer to the body is plain). The treatment ends with another row of narrow insertion and a ruffle of the lace edging.

The back fastens with four tiny Dorset buttons in the bodice, and a 1-inch wide band of batiste extends at waist level from side seams to center back, with rows of stitching forming five tiny drawstring casings. Only two tiny tape ties remain; but originally, the five sets of drawstrings would have made a pretty gathered back, echoing the pintucks of the skirt. The dress is entirely French-seamed; it is 42-inches long overall with a skirt circumference of 75-inches.

99.39.3 Gift of Ann Robinson King and Mrs. Samuel Fletcher King, Jr. in memory of Mary Jane Robinson Williamson

Ayrshire Work TODDLER DRESS

1850s

"It is quite unnecessary to make tacks in the skirt, except for ornament; as, just in proportion as the child grows taller, the skirts are made shorter; but with the body it is different. The waist requires to be lengthened, and the armholes and back let out. The seams at the shoulders and under the arms should be folded in, so that an inch can be let out in each one…. By attending to this, the dress that is made for a child of one year old will fit him until he is three."
—Godey's Ladies' Book, August 1857

The bodice on this little dress may have been made from an infant's gown, to which a new skirt was attached. Both the Ayrshire embroidery in the central V-shaped bodice panel and the embroidered flanges are similar to the Ayrshire infants' gowns elsewhere in this book.

Like most of these mid-century infant and toddlers' gowns, this one has large side seam allowances, 2-inches deep on each side of each hem, so that as Godey's informed the sewing mother of 1857, "the dress that is made for a child of one…will fit him until he is three."

The bodice features exquisite Ayrshire-embroidered panels, with a band of embroidery between two rows of eyelets bordering the V-shape. The embroidery of both the waistband and the bodice flanges is among the most elaborate that can be found in Ayrshire work. The short sleeves are topped with crescent-shaped caps, embroidered with a scalloped eyelet edge and more Ayrshire work; the sleeve is edged in the same scalloped eyelet design.

The skirt is simple, gauged into the waistband and finished with seven rows of 1/4-inch tucks and a 2-1/2-inch hem. Although both the bodice and skirt may have been made with growth in mind, no alterations appear to have been made, except possibly for the alteration from infancy to older babyhood.

53.153 *Gift of Grace Pelton Holbert*

DAR MUSEUM

"... a skeleton suit, one of those straight blue cloth cases in which small boys used to be confined, before belts and tunics had come in, and old notions had gone out: an ingenious contrivance for displaying the full symmetry of a boy's figure, by fastening him into a very tight jacket, with an ornamental row of buttons over each shoulder, and then buttoning his trousers over it, so as to give his legs the appearance of being hooked on, just under the armpits."

–CHARLES DICKENS, *Sketches by Boz*, 1836

John Briggs's BLUE SKELETON SUIT

1822

The cross-stitched "Family Record" of the Briggs family of Sumner, Maine tells the sad story behind this skeleton suit. Family history recorded that Lydia Winslow Briggs spun and wove the striped blue linen in 1822 and made it into this little suit for her not quite 3-year-old son John, born in September 1819. This would have been his first pair of trousers after wearing frocks as a baby and toddler. The transition to trousers, called "breeching" even after men's breeches had been superseded by trousers, was a momentous event for both boy and mother—the latter often shedding a tear or two for the passing of babyhood. Even more sadly, little John died the same summer as he was breeched, just two weeks short of his third birthday, and the skeleton suit was put away and saved through many later generations in the family. The Family Record lists John's birth and death and the birth in 1824 of another son, also named John—a common practice from colonial days into the early 19th century.

The "skeleton" suit was meant to be a playsuit, reflecting a shift in attitudes towards children in the late 18th century, which understood and encouraged the need for play. It appears to have gotten its name from the form-fitting nature of the style. Earlier versions of the skeleton suit were trimmed with military-style braid across the chest along with the buttons, imitating Hussar cavalry uniforms, which may also have suggested ribs of a skeleton. (See the white Young Boy's Skeleton Suit elsewhere in this book for an example with buttons.)

This example has a raised waistline typical of skeleton suits, which reflected the high waists in women's fashions of the day. Unusually, it does not have buttons in front and fastens in back with 10 round brass shank buttons securing a drop-back bottom. Unlike some suits, which were made in two overlapping pieces, this one is a one-piece garment. To assist little John with calls of nature, there is a discreet little opening in the center front seam near the top of the trousers.

91.269.1 *Friends of the Museum Purchase*

DAR MUSEUM

Gathered Bodice SUMMER DRESS

About 1850

"Almost every description of toilette worn by grown-up persons is made on a reduced scale for little girls, and most of them look very pretty."
—*Peterson's Magazine*, December 1864

This summer dress of about 1850 mimics adult fashion, while simplifying it, as many American mothers thought appropriate for children. Its high, slightly V-shaped, piped neckline, pleating at the shoulders to create the bodice fullness, and bias-cut bodice front are all modified versions of ladies' dresses of the 1840s and 1850s. An adult woman's waistline would have been pointed, so the straight line here, although piped like a lady's bodice edge, is a concession to childhood. The bodice is lined in a slightly heavier fabric.

The skirt is decorated at the hem with an inch-deep tuck, an insertion band with embroidered and eyelet flowers between two sets of pintucks barely 1/8-inch deep, and finally with an embroidered and scalloped hem. Satin-stitch leaves and eyelet and embroidered floral sprays adorn each scallop. The insertion and scalloped edging were store-bought. The sleeves are edged with a band of the same embroidery as embellishes the area between the pintucks on the skirt, and additionally with a ruffle of needle-run lace with a scalloped edge. The dress fastens in back with five hooks and eyes.

76.101 DAR Museum

DAR MUSEUM

Broderie Anglaise
GIRL'S DRESS

1850s

"Girls in white dresses with blue satin sashes…these are a few of my favorite things."
—RODGERS AND HAMMERSTEIN, *The Sound of Music*

Dramatic broderie anglaise of the 1850s enlivens this otherwise demure white cotton dress, originally worn by Amanda Bacon of Booneville, Missouri. A narrow strip of broderie anglaise at the neckline forms the shoulder strap, and the short, gathered cap sleeves are sewn into this band. As the neckline is backed with plain cotton, it is probable that blue ribbon to match the waistband once was threaded behind the eyelets.

The sleeves are edged with 1-inch diameter compass work (overlapping circles) of eyelet embroidery, forming a scalloped edge. The simple, gathered bodice is entirely plain, the only touch of color provided by an eyelet waistband through which a blue silk-satin ribbon is threaded. The full skirt is gauged into the bottom of the waistband. It is edged with large-scale concentric circles of more broderie anglaise, forming a scalloped hem beneath three decorative pleats. That this would have been Miss Amanda's "best dress" is evident not only from the copious handwork that went into decorating it, but also by the low neckline, which was, by this time, only used for special-occasion clothing.

47.39 *Gift of the Elizabeth Benton Chapter*

DAR MUSEUM

Eva May Ratcliffe's
DROP-WAIST DRESS

1880s

"White muslin dresses have superseded the stiff piqué and Marseilles Gabrielles formerly worn by very small girls. The yoke slips and sacque dresses, either pleated or plain of white nansook, provided for the first short clothes, furnish designs for these up to four or five years of age."
—HARPER'S BAZAR, "New York Fashions," November 30, 1878

The hip-length waistline, short gathered skirt, and narrow sleeves of this sweet little dress place it in the early 1880s, as does its history. Little Eva May Ratcliffe, born in 1877, wore this as a girl of about 3 or 4 years old in Illinois. Vertical panels of cotton with five pleats each alternate with needle-run cotton lace, 1-1/4-inches wide. The sleeves echo this, with one row of insertion between panels of three pleats each. The skirt repeats this pattern horizontally below a short band of gathered cotton, with a row of insertion, a row of pleated cotton, and finally a row of lace edging. The same edging finishes the sleeves and forms a collar. The back fastens with seven buttons, only one of which, a diamond-shaped milk glass button, remains.

95.85.2 *Gift of Rhyllis Rae Oedekoven*

44 | DAR MUSEUM

DAR MUSEUM

Linen BOY'S JACKET

Late 1850s

"Children's Fashions. General Remarks…Sacques are the popular out-of-door garment…"
—*Peterson's Magazine*, May 1864

Harvey Glidden, born in the late 1850s, was a toddler when he wore this little tan linen jacket. The style imitates the ladies' sacque jackets popular at the time, the name deriving from their loose, unstructured lines. Instead of the more typical flat braid trim known as soutache, seen in Harvey's red and black dress elsewhere in this book, a chain stitched leafy vine was sewn by hand along the front, bottom and sleeve edges. A narrow band collar of the same linen fastens with a Dorset button. The scalloped edges of the jacket are finished by hand with buttonhole stitch. The seams are hand sewn in back stitch.

4099 Gift of Mrs. Harry L. Glidden

DAR MUSEUM

Harvey Glidden's RED DRESS

Early 1860s

"…. The richest and prettiest is braid, worked in handsome patterns."
"THE DRESS OF CHILDREN. TRIMMING." *Godey's Ladies' Book,* May 1857

It is often said that "they used to dress boys as girls," but Victorians used many clues to "read" a toddler's gender. We know this dress was worn by young Harvey Glidden, born in about 1857-58. His linen jacket is also pictured in this book. The vibrant red color would have been considered sufficiently masculine, and the black "soutache" braid applied trim sports a leafy, not feminine, floral motif. Even so, since the Victorians did not consider very young children to have highly developed gender identities, Harvey's sister could have worn this, if he had one. The trousers Harvey would have worn underneath would have been plainer than a girl's pantalettes, and his hair would have been parted at the side, like a man; whereas girls wore theirs parted in the middle.

This dress shows construction and decoration typical of the mid-19th century in its plain square torso, short sleeves, low neck and gathered skirt. The neckline is bound with plain-weave binding, which was probably black and has faded to brown. Six black crocheted buttons fasten the dress at center back. The waistband is outlined top and bottom with narrow velvet trim, and a second soutache motif, of a stylized fleur de lys in swags, edges the short sleeves, which are topped with double puffs. The skirt is gathered onto the waistband, and beneath the black soutache trim is a decorative tuck; the skirt has a typically generous 2-inch hem. Skirt tucks are often assumed to be added to allow for growth, but they are more frequently merely decorative. By the time Harvey needed the extra length, he would have been old enough to graduate to trousers.

4097 Gift of Mrs. Harry L. Glidden

DAR MUSEUM

Raglan Sleeve MUSLIN DRESS

About 1845

"We cannot enforce more earnestly than is necessary, perfect simplicity in the dress of children. They are not puppets, made for the display of fine clothes; or Paris dolls, to be tricked out in the extravagance of the latest fashion. We give a report of what may be worn; but every mother should be guided by her means, her time, and the health of her infant."

—GODEY'S LADIES' BOOK, July 1850

Sometimes family history attached to a garment does not match what the garment can "tell" us about its history. The donor of this dress believed it had been made in 1821, but its style belongs to the 1840s or '50s, with its simple bodice ending at a natural waist level, wide square neckline, and short sleeves. Perhaps the fabric was reused from an earlier child's dress, as the sheer cotton is embroidered mull muslin of the kind imported from India in the early 19th century and used on women and children's dresses alike.

The sheer muslin is backed in the bodice with heavier white cotton. The bodice ties at the neckline in back and closes with six crocheted buttons down the rest of the bodice. The raglan sleeves are made of machine-embroidered sheer lace, with floral and vine motifs and a pointed scalloped edge, the points filled with French knots. The waist seam is self-piped. An embroidered vine motif wends its way around the bottom of the bodice.

47.95 Gift of Mary E. Rawson

DAR MUSEUM

Appliquéd Floral EMBROIDERED DRESS

Between 1845-1865

"You mothers who love the bright little girls, whose very lives are bound up in the happiness of your children, does it ever occur to you that you are doing too much for them in this matter? -hours sometimes spent in fanciful embroidery or superfluous tucks, puffs and lace trimmings, things which usually foster vanity in your children and jealousy in their playmates, while often the affections and minds of the little ones are in need of counsel and guidance."

–NEW YORK EVANGELIST, "The Children of the Household," Jan. 16, 1890

With the advent of machinery that could not only weave fabric, but could even imitate handwork, embellished garments would no longer be the luxury items of the few who had the leisure to make or money to buy them. This child's dress is decorated with an appliquéd floral spray that was machine-embroidered and store-bought, and hand-stitched to the bodice. A waistband of Swiss embroidery (backed, somewhat surprisingly, with pale orange pinstriped printed cotton), and the sleeve and neck edging of sheer cotton with scalloped embroidered borders, make this heavy ribbed cotton dress nearly as elaborate as the hand-embroidered Ayrshire dresses it attempts to imitate. A full skirt is gauged into the waistband: tiny pleats are stacked on top of each other, fastened by whipstitching one edge of each pleat to the waistband. The back fastens with ties.

6931 Gift of Emeline A. Street

DAR MUSEUM

Late Victorian GIRL'S DRESS

About 1890

> "There are few changes in fashion of garments for little folks. American mothers have very conservative taste in this regard, and generally prefer plain English styles to the elaborate French ones. The length of the skirt is more a matter of taste than fashion, and depends more upon the size than the age. Tiny tots of two or three years, are covered to the feet; for a girl of eight the frocks should reach only a few inches below the knee, and should increase in length with advancing year until at twelve they should reach the ankle."
>
> –"LATEST FASHIONS," *The Ladies' Home Journal*, May 1890

Victorians, eager to preserve childhood as a time of innocence, dressed young girls in garments that de-emphasized, or even ignored, areas of the body accentuated in the womanly figure, namely waist, chest and hips. Thus, very young girls of the 1880s and 1890s wore dresses with no waistline at all, and slightly older girls wore drop-waisted dresses.

The yoke of this charming batiste dress of about 1890 alternates bands of machine embroidery with vertical tucks. Puffed sleeves are topped with ruffles at the shoulder and end at the elbow with ruffles edged with openwork and embroidery. The body of the dress is shirred in two rows of gathers at the front, with a ruffle heading overlapping the bottom of the yoke. The waistband is made of the same embroidered band as is used on the yoke. The body, yoke and sleeves are made of a lighter cotton than the skirt, which has a machine-embroidered edge resembling, but different from, the embroidery elsewhere. The dress fastens in back with different arrangements for the yoke and the body of the dress. On the yoke, the buttons are sewn on the underside of the right side of the opening and face toward the body; on the body of the dress, the buttons are on the left side and face outward, but are hidden by the placket.

4694.1 Gift of Mrs. G. J. Nickerson

DAR MUSEUM

Princess Panel TODDLER'S DRESS

1880s

T he high neck of this little dress reflects the rejection of the earlier theory that children's necklines should be low, exposing their chests to "harden" them against catching colds. Although Godey's, the popular ladies' fashion magazine, warned against this theory as early as the 1850s, it was not until about 1870 that children's necklines rose significantly. Parents of the last third of the 19th century finally preferred to protect their children from cold, and dressed them in high-necked garments. This pretty little dress echoes women's fashion of the 1880s, with its princess-style panel down the front. The panel alternates 1-1/2-inches wide strips of ruching with horizontal bands of machine lace in a variation on a Greek key motif. The lace reappears on the edges of the long sleeves and above the skirt hem. The long sleeves are piped at the armscye and have a deep cuff consisting of a band of the Greek key trim, a band of shirring, and a scalloped edging matching that at the neckline.

The skirt's hem is decorated with a band of the Greek key trim, a band of shirring, and a deep edging of exquisite handmade Ayrshire-style whitework and eyelet embroidery. It has a classical acanthus-leaf central design repeating above an elaborate scalloped edge, with needle-lace-filled eyelets and smaller plain eyelets all about. The dress opens all the way down the back, fastening with nine large shell buttons.

4694.2 *Gift of Mrs. G. J. Nickerson*

> "It is a vulgar error to suppose that children should be left bare as to their legs, their chest, and arms…the truth is that more children die through the stupidity of their parents…than from any single disease which can be mentioned."
>
> –GODEY'S LADIES' BOOK,
> September 1857

Pink Cotton SMOCKED DRESS

1920s

"Children's clothes should be made very simply. Use a good quality material and suitably childish colors. The one-piece dress is an accepted style for small boys and girls, and can be made of wool, linen or cotton materials."

–THE DRESSMAKER, Butterick Publishing Co., 1916

This lightweight pink cotton dress of the 1920s has a center-front slit edged with bias tape and ties at the neck with the same tape. A falling collar is decorated with a scalloped edge and satin-stitch embroidery. The body is cut in one piece, with just one seam at the left side. Two pockets were created by cutting slits in the front and placing pockets of the same fabric behind them, then adding flaps, which are decorated with embroidery to match the collar. A double layer of fabric is inserted at the shoulder to form a small yoke. The edges of the shoulder yoke pieces are self-piped, and there is smocking beneath the yoke at front and back. The armscye is also piped and bound on the inside with bias tape. Short puffed sleeves with turned-up cuffs are decorated with the same embroidered edging as the collar and the pocket flaps. Not surprisingly, as the label proclaims "Made in France," this little jacket is completely French seamed.

92.301.2 DAR Museum

DAR MUSEUM

Faux Needlepoint WOOL DRESS

1840s

"Little girls, you will not be willing to spend all your time in amusing yourselves, I am sure. You wish to be useful. Well, this is the time for you to learn to knit and sew. The weather is neither too cold nor too warm. Sit down by your mother or sister and be very patient and careful, and you will soon learn."

—THE YOUTH'S COMPANION, "The Nursery," Dec. 3, 1841

Although this dear little dress has been fiddled with, and its sleeves and gathers no longer present their original appearance, its charm is scarcely diminished. At some point in time the waist gathers were either deliberately let out, or came undone, resulting in an uneven appearance. The cheerful turquoise blue wool blend is set off by multi-colored floral embroidery at the edges of both sleeves and skirt. The embroidery resembles Berlin work, or what we would now call needlepoint, except that it is embroidered on the wool, not on a canvas grid.

The bodice and skirt of this dress are actually constructed of one piece, with gathers at the waist creating the effect of two separate pieces. More gathers are found at the neck, and the sleeves are set in at the sides. Woven tapes inside the dress stabilize the gathers at both waist and the front of the neckline. (The back neckline, which has only one row of gathers, does not have woven tape.) The neckline is bound with bias bands of the same wool as the dress. The seams on the bottom and top of the cuffs of both sets of sleeves, as well as the long sleeve's lengthwise seam, are piped. The longer sleeve pieces have been shortened, as their length, when set under the upper sleeves, does not seem sufficient to create full-length sleeves. Originally they would have been under the shorter sleeves, and the two-tiered sleeves would have echoed sleeves popular in women's dresses of the 1840s. They are lined in cotton muslin and have gathers at the inner elbows to give some ease of movement. Conceivably, they were always detached, and were stitched in as needed allowing wear in both warm and cold weather. Children's clothes were frequently reused by younger siblings, so sleeves might be attached, detached, and reattached several times within the lifetime of the garment.

74.13.1-2 *Gift of Mrs. Count R. Boyd*

Young Boy's SKELETON SUIT

About 1825-1835

"This little appendage is usually the first change the parents give their children, when they are tired of seeing them in frocks, and we think as easy and simple (well made) as any thing that can be substituted.... the most ridiculous are those that are made after the manner of grown up people, with Coat, Waistcoat and Breeches, making them appear like dwarfs, or little old men."
—THE TAYLOR'S COMPLETE GUIDE, 1796

The trouser suit, known as a "skeleton suit," was the first style made for young boys that was not a miniature of an adult style. It entered fashion in the late 1770s, reflecting the new attitudes towards children that acknowledged their need to play, and for clothes that allowed them freedom of motion. This little outfit dates to the 1820s or early 1830s, as we can tell from the puffy sleeves that echo women's sleeves of that time. Young boys' as well as girls' clothing often incorporated elements borrowed from women's dress. As boys got older, their clothes were modeled increasingly on menswear.

The suit is made of sturdy plain white cotton, which may seem impractical, but it could be scoured and bleached; it may also represent a slightly dressier version of the style. The puffed sleeves are cartridge pleated into the armscyes, with semi-circular gussets under the arms. The trousers have a fly opening in the crotch seam—boys were not put into trousers until they were out of diapers. There is also a 1-inch deep decorative pleat immediately above the hem of the trouser legs.

White glass buttons are used extensively, both decoratively and functionally. They fasten the top or bodice to the trousers all around the waist (hidden by the cotton waistband), but the back opening of the bodice closes with hooks and eyes, with five decorative buttons down center back. The trousers open at the side seams with three buttons below the waist fastening, of which only the top two are functional. The buttons on the bodice front are purely decorative.

The only other decoration on this little suit is subtle: double rows of narrow white cotton twill tape, which trim the leg pleats, trouser hem and sleeve cuff. They surround the rows of buttons on the bodice and side seams, and follow the seams in back of the bodice. A single row of the same tape trims the top and bottom edges of the waistband.

2001.59 Friends of the Museum Purchase

DAR MUSEUM

Checked Weave EVERYDAY PINAFORE

Mid-19th Century

"Ethel was a little girl about eleven years old, who liked to keep herself beautifully neat and clean. You never saw her with rough hair, or untidy pinafore, or dirty hands; and as for tearing her frock, most likely she never did such a thing in all her life."

–ELIZA STEPHENSON, *Sunnyland Stories*, 1876

Garments that were anything but "best" are much less often saved, and therefore are welcomed by grateful curators and collectors as rare survivals of the wear and tear of childhood. This sweet little pinafore is simply made from cotton with a tiny woven check created by the use of slightly thicker threads about every five threads in both warp and weft. The two rounded V-shaped bodice pieces are sewn in front and back to the waistband, and seamed to each other at the shoulder. The bodice pieces are unlined and finished with a rolled hem. The skirt, 10-1/2-inches long, extends only slightly beyond the side of the body, and is shirred into the waistband, which is lined with muslin.

3781.9 *Gift of Mrs. Guy C. Lamson*

Ice-Blue Satin QUILTED PETTICOAT

1760-1780

Palest ice-blue silk satin is used in this lovely quilted petticoat of the third quarter of the 18th century. The pleats, which face towards the back, gather 129-inches of circumference into a 26-1/2-inch linen waistband. The petticoat opens at the left and has two linen tape ties. The upper 20-1/2-inches are quilted in a 1/2-inch grid pattern set on point (on the diagonal). At the base of the petticoat is an elaborate design featuring stylized leaves, flowers and feather motifs, the upper part alternating trefoils over triangles between arcs enclosing feather designs. At the hem, a serpentine vine motif winds around the placement of half-flowers. The petticoat's edge is bound in palest blue silk ribbon. The backing is linen and the filling, cotton. The quilting motifs resemble French quilting of this era, but English petticoats with similar designs also survive, indicating the constant exchange of designs between the two countries. Although some colonial Americans quilted petticoats for themselves, this type of garment was one of the earliest to be imported as a "readymade" item for sale in a shop, and needed only to be pleated onto the waistband of the buyer.

78.48 DAR Museum

"To whomever gave the well-quilted petticoat please say that Aunt Ann has bespoken for them an extra-heavy crown 'ob hebenly glory.'"

–ANECDOTICAL AND MISCELLANEOUS, "A Good Samaritan in Virginia,"
Lippincott's Magazine of Popular Literature and Science, July 1881

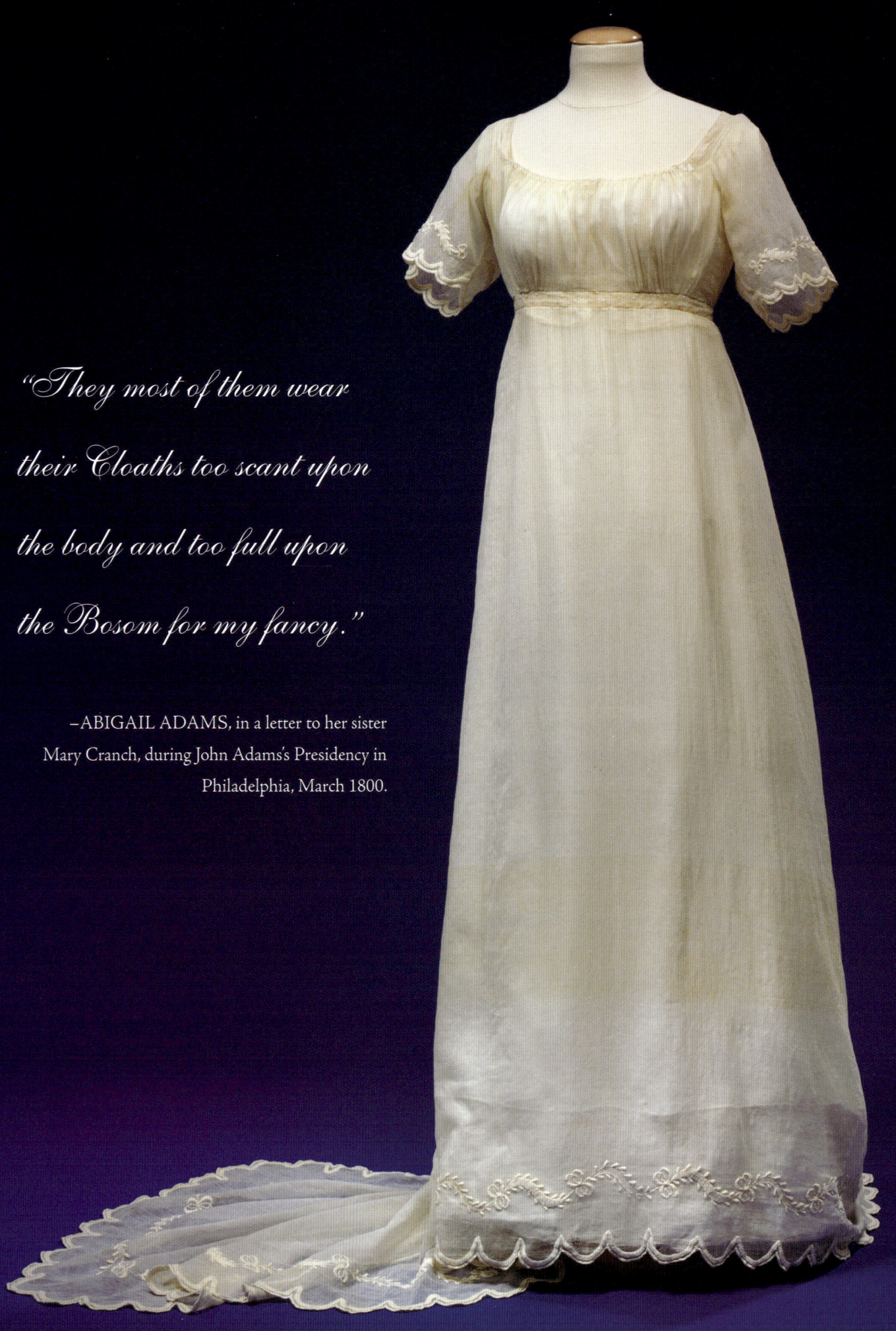

"They most of them wear their Cloaths too scant upon the body and too full upon the Bosom for my fancy."

—ABIGAIL ADAMS, in a letter to her sister Mary Cranch, during John Adams's Presidency in Philadelphia, March 1800.

Embroidered Transparent MUSLIN GOWN

1800-1805

Sheer white dresses were the height of fashion at the turn of the 19th century in Europe, and the finest were made of pre-embroidered cotton imported from India. Americans were ambivalent about the new style; it could be worn with the barest minimum of undergarments, and the soft fabric tended to cling to the female form. Compared to the stately styles of the previous century, these seemed positively "naked." Nevertheless, the young and fashionable, perhaps primarily in the cities, dared to appear at formal functions in the latest rage.

This dress is an excellent example of the cutting edge of feminine fashion in 1800-05, with transparent Indian "mull" muslin—the term muslin meaning a much softer fabric than it does today—embroidered at the hem and sleeve edges with a delicate design in heavier white cotton thread. The fabric would have been embroidered in India, designed to be made up into dresses in Europe or America. The hem and sleeves have embroidered scalloped edging. A few inches above this are graceful undulations of bow knots between leafy sprigs.

The bodice is constructed with a simply gathered front panel with a scoop neck, underarm panels, two back panels, and narrow shoulder pieces connecting the front and back bodice pieces. A 3/4-inch waistband lined in linen joins bodice and skirt. The skirt's front panel is virtually straight in front, without gathering. To avoid bunching over the stomach and hips, the fabric has been slit for about 2-inches at center front and hiked up, to taper towards the side seams. The extra fabric has been folded under the skirt; it is just visible under the waistband at the front. As with all dresses of this time, the fullness of the dress is concentrated at the back with 38-inches of fabric gathered into just a few inches at the center back. Side panels are 3-inches wide at the waistband, widening to 18-inches at the hem. The train has a squared edge and is 32-inches long.

79.12.1 Gift of the Morristown Chapter

Center Panel Embroidery
MULL GOWN

1800-1805

Neoclassical dresses would seem to be a good match for the neoclassical taste in architecture and furniture, since they all copied European styles, and also alluded to America's government based on Greek democracy and the Roman republic. But in fact, the sheer, clinging fabrics shocked most Americans. The high-waisted, slim-skirted European styles were adopted in the young United States, but usually in less transparent fabrics. Nevertheless, some fashionable ladies—mostly the young and slender, in cities accustomed to following the latest and most extreme fashion whims—dared to appear at elegant functions in the thin Indian cottons, braving the criticism of their elders.

This dress is an example of imported mull muslin, on to which the embroidery has been executed with a trained gown in mind, as it extends down the center front of the skirt and around a predetermined hem and 24-inch train. The maker of the dress had only to cut off the skirt at the height required to fit the intended wearer; the excess embroidery is visible in the seams of the garment. The embroidered stylized leafy sprigs form a panel, 5-inches wide on the skirt and 4-1/2-inches deep around the hem. The bodice and sleeves are not embroidered. The bodice is gently gathered in front and back, with a drawstring extending all around the neckline, tying at center back. The waistline fastens with a hook and eye at center back. The bodice is lined in white cotton in front and at the sides, but is unlined in the back panels.

76.103 DAR Museum

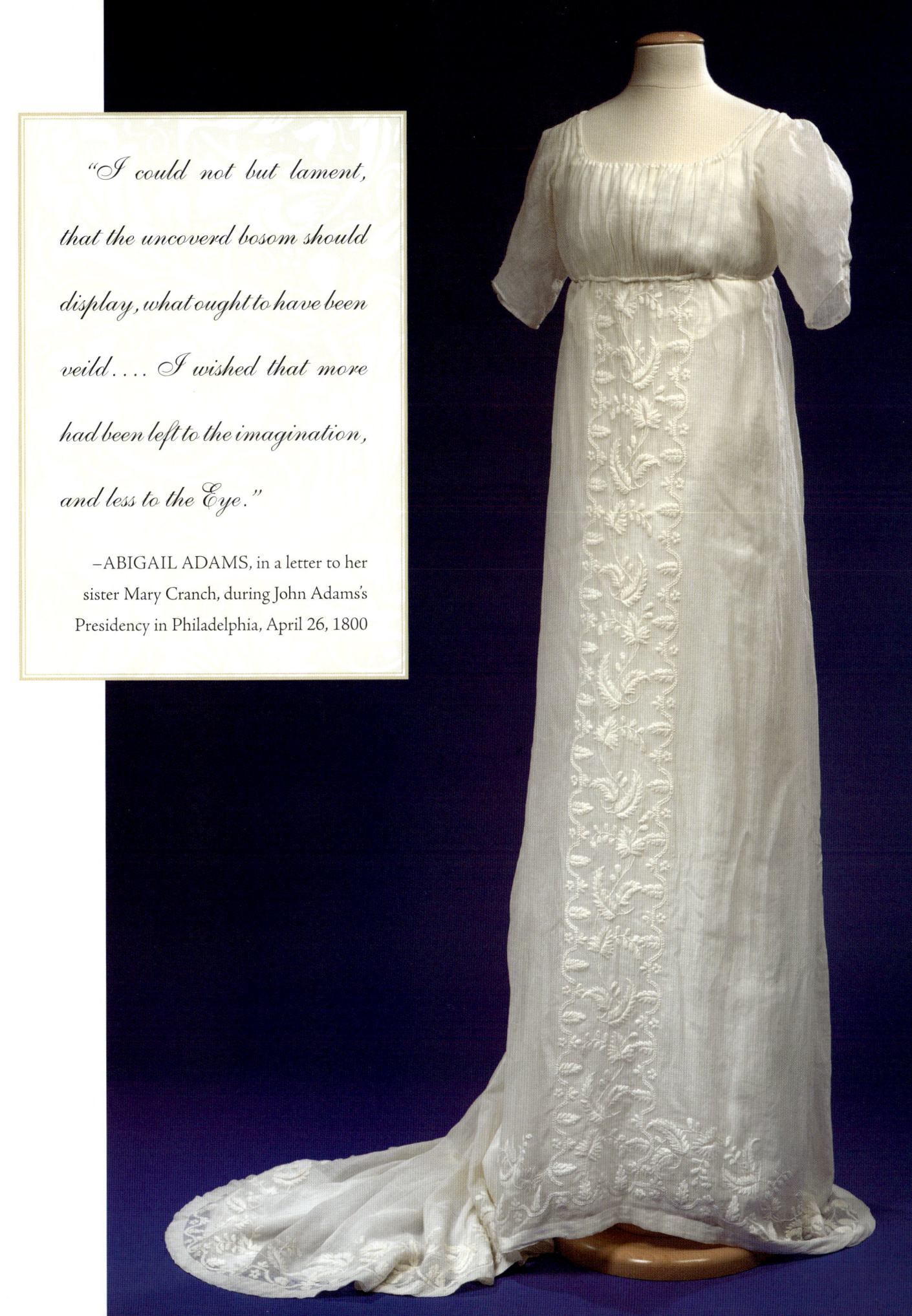

"*I could not but lament, that the uncoverd bosom should display, what ought to have been veild.... I wished that more had been left to the imagination, and less to the Eye.*"

—ABIGAIL ADAMS, in a letter to her sister Mary Cranch, during John Adams's Presidency in Philadelphia, April 26, 1800

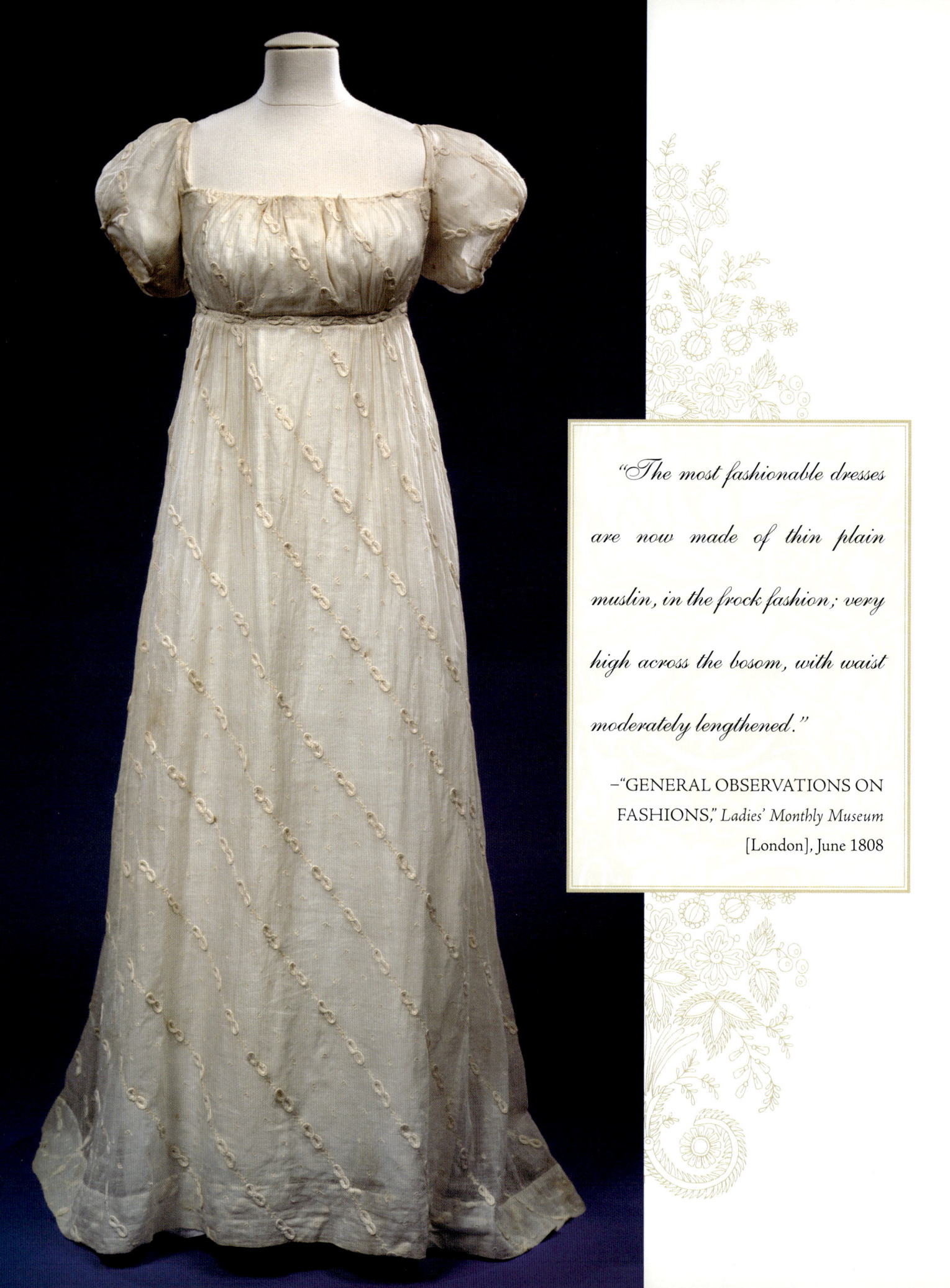

"*The most fashionable dresses are now made of thin plain muslin, in the frock fashion; very high across the bosom, with waist moderately lengthened.*"

–"GENERAL OBSERVATIONS ON FASHIONS," *Ladies' Monthly Museum* [London], June 1808

Neoclassical Mull DRAWSTRING GOWN

1806-1812

The lack of a train on this simple dress helps us date it to slightly after 1806, when trains went out of fashion. It indicates the continued popularity of the neoclassical white cotton dress for girls and young ladies at the turn of the century, despite some critics' complaints at the "nakedness" of the clinging muslins and low necklines. It fastens in back, and would thus have been called a "frock." There is also a drawstring at the center front neckline to adjust the fit. After about 1810, the frock style became increasingly popular.

The fabric is soft, sheer Indian cotton, a mull muslin—very different from what we call muslin today. It was embroidered in India with heavier cotton thread in parallel diagonal lines of figure eights and small floral sprigs.

The construction of the dress is typically simple for this period. The skirt, 93-inches in diameter, is made of straight panels at front and back, barely gathered in front with most of the fullness gathered into the center back. Triangular panels at the sides give more fullness at the hem without additional gathers at the waist. The waistband and bodice were originally fully lined in white cotton; all but the lining in the waistband and underarm panels have been removed. The dress fastens with a drawstring at the back neckline and a hook and eye at the waist.

57.5 Gift of Captain Molly Pitcher Chapter

Ruched Bodice
EVENING GOWN

About 1820

"Muslin is at present the most fashionable material for dinner dress. The bodies of gowns are made plain, with short sleeves, richly trimmed with lace. The bottom of the skirts are very richly embroidered."
–LADIES' MONTHLY MUSEUM [London], July 1818

The bodice front and sleeves of this dress are constructed from alternating bands of ruched sheer muslin and net lace insertions. Four 3-1/2-inch wide panels of muslin gathered along the edges form ruched panels, which alternate with 1-inch-wide hand-embroidered net lace. The only shoulder piece connecting front and back bodices, into which the sleeves are sewn, are strips of the net lace. The sides of the bodice front panel and the bodice back, are plain pieces of the muslin, as are the underneath parts of the sleeves. The waist has a single drawstring all around the body tying at the back. The neckline has one drawstring at front, from sleeves to center front, and another in the back, from each sleeve to center back.

The construction of the skirt shows the development from the straight slim skirts of the first decade of the century to the widening skirts of the teens. It is made of four gored panels: from waistline to hem, the front panel tapers from 16-1/4- to 31-inches; the side panels taper from a mere 1-1/2- to 9-inches; the back panel is 35-inches wide, gathered at the waist into 14-1/2-inches.

According to the donor, this dress was worn by a member of the Lockwood family of Connecticut and New York.

93.25 *Gift of Margaret Close*

DAR MUSEUM

Purple Velvet
SPENCER JACKET

About 1818

Picture a Jane Austen heroine in this little velvet jacket. Its details allow us to date it fairly precisely to about 1818, and we know it to have been worn by a member of Abigail Adams's family, probably a granddaughter. These short jackets reached to the fashionably high waists of the period, and were known as "spencers." This name is, probably apocryphally, attributed to the 2nd Earl Spencer (brother of the glamorous fashion leader Georgiana, Duchess of Devonshire, and an ancestor of Diana, Princess of Wales) who supposedly cut the tails off his coat when they got torn on the hunting field—or possibly singed at the fireside, as a different legend has it. Whatever its origin, American women as well as English ones wore the latest variations on the style from the late 1790s into the 1820s. They would have been useful in cold weather, worn over the thin fashionable cottons of the time, and provided a colorful accent.

In the late 1810s, historic periods and military uniforms inspired ladies' fashions. In this rich plum velvet version, vaguely Renaissance- or Cavalier-era-style puffed sleeves of purple twilled silk, each puff punctuated with three velvet button-centered twill rosettes, are mixed with military-inspired trim on the front of the jacket. Continuous tubes of the twill (like cording, but hollow) veer back and forth across the chest, accented by 20 velvet-covered buttons at the outer edges, imitating the trim on jackets worn by Hussar troops. These Hungarian cavalry officers were renowned as much for their costly and dashing uniforms as for their military prowess, and by the time of the Napoleonic wars, all the European allies had created their own Hussar troops. Their elaborately trimmed jackets were copied and echoed in men, women and even children's fashions of the early 1800s. (See the skeleton suits elsewhere in this book.)

The Spencer fastens with concealed hooks and eyes, allowing edge-to-edge closure at center front. A separately cut velvet collar is decorated with silk trim in a looping pattern to echo the Hussar trim, and more tubing outlines the curved seams on the back of the bodice. The collar edge and shoulder seams are piped in the same twilled silk. The sleeves are extra long and slightly flared at the wrist, intended to go over the hand. The entire spencer is lined with a gray and white striped silk with a 3/4-inch wide black silk lining at the waist.

4728 Gift of Elizabeth S. Garfield

"Cloaks now wholly disappeared, and given place to Spencers of every description, but the most fashionable is the military Spencer made of velvet..."

–LADY'S MAGAZINE
(London), November 1803

DAR MUSEUM

Catherine Burroughs's
PUFFED HEM DRESS

Mid-1820s

The elaborate treatment of the bodice and hem on this dress, and its waistline and full skirt, reflect the departure from the pure neoclassical style of 1800. As fashion must always change, the slim, high-waisted styles evolved into widening skirts and lowering waistlines. Hems and bodices were embellished with increasingly elaborate trim. This sweet design, with its waist still slightly above the natural level, was worn about 1824 by Catherine Burroughs of Bridgeport, Connecticut.

The bodice, which fastens in back with hooks and eyes, features alternating bands of shirring and embroidery with piping separating each band; the back bodice seams are also piped. Its wide, shirred neckline is made from sheerer cotton than the rest of the dress, with a 1-inch band of stylized, floral motifs that include eyelets and satin-stitch leaves with silk net filling the center flower. The embroidery is worked on the same fabric as the rest of the dress. The bodice front has another repeat of the shirred lawn and

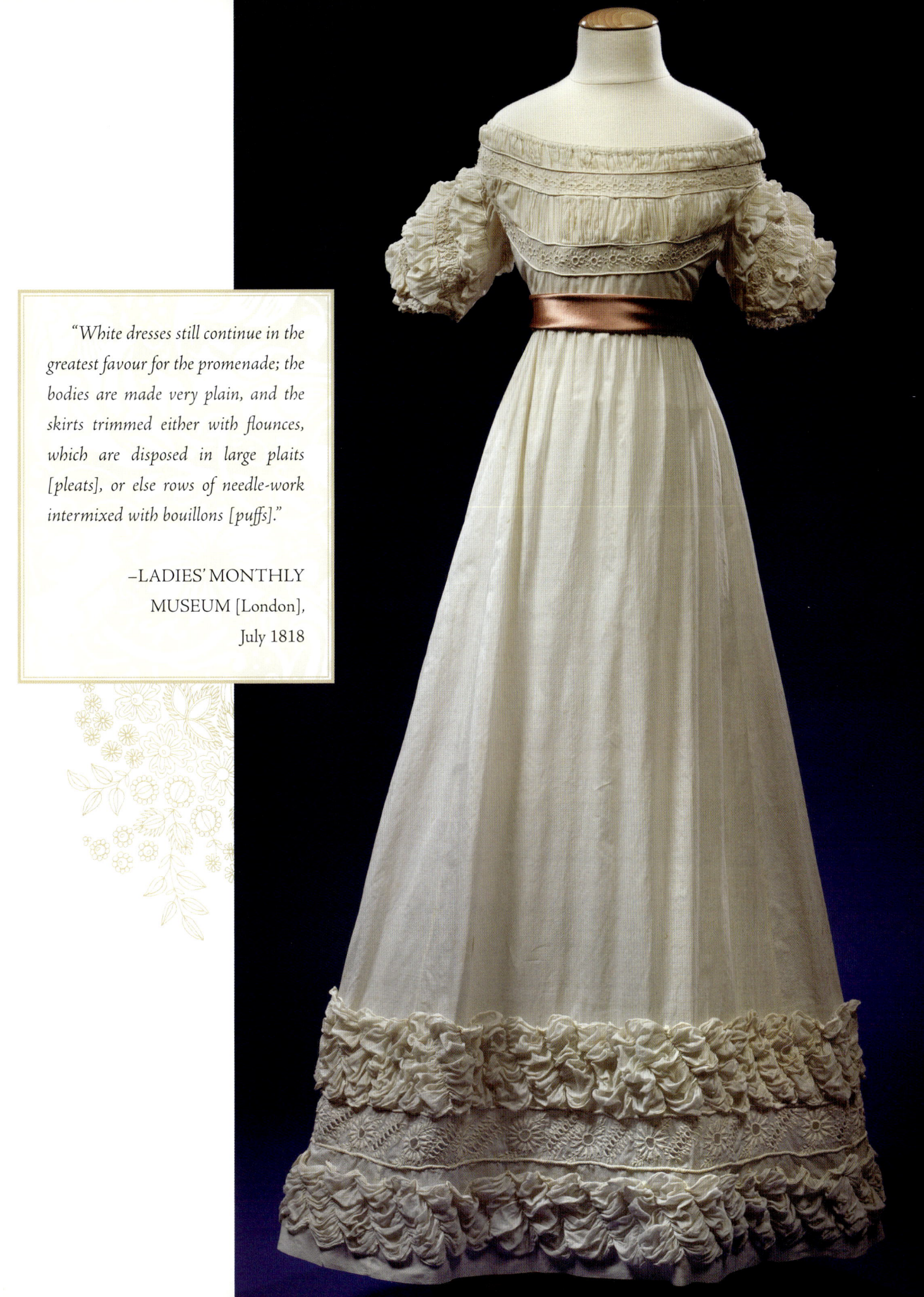

"White dresses still continue in the greatest favour for the promenade; the bodies are made very plain, and the skirts trimmed either with flounces, which are disposed in large plaits [pleats], or else rows of needle-work intermixed with bouillons [puffs]."

–LADIES' MONTHLY MUSEUM [London], July 1818

the embroidered band, while the back has only one band of each. Two darts extend from the bottom of the second embroidered band to the waistband. The bodice is lined in the back and at the sides with white linen, leaving the front unlined and diaphanous.

The short sleeves echo the bodice's decoration, but its shirred panels are separate pieces of cotton applied to the sleeve above its ground fabric. Four diagonal bands each of shirring and embroidery to match that of the bodice, also piped at every edge, alternate around the sleeves; the underside of the arm is plain. Piping also edges the armscye, and the sleeve openings have a narrow Vandyked (pointed scalloped) edging with trefoil satin-stitch leaves above each Vandyke.

At the hem, which is 85-inches in circumference, two 3-1/2-inch wide rows of applied shirring are separated by a 2-inch wide band of openwork embroidery. The shirring is made of a bias band of muslin (the same as the dress) 11-inches wide with diagonal rows of basting stitches gathering the muslin, after which it is tacked to the skirt 2-inches apart. The design of the embroidered band, also made of the fabric of the dress, is reminiscent of the bodice and sleeve motif, but larger in scale and more elaborate. Its flowers variously have 14 or 15 petals, and a center of net. The skirt is cut with two side gores, which widen from 2-inches (sewn into 1-1/2-inches of the bodice) to 12-inches at the hem, giving the skirt its fashionable triangular shape.

6864 Gift of Marion Hallam Waller

DAR MUSEUM

Lady's Unfinished NET COLLAR

1830s

This unfinished collar offers insight into the way needlewomen planned and executed their projects and is more interesting than it would be if finished. Every stage of the project is illustrated. First, the machine-made cotton net was basted to five layers of paper from the account book of David Chauncey of Bath, Maine (this information and the date of the transactions, 1833, are visible on the pages). On the top layer, an embroidery design was drawn in ink. Then, fine cotton lawn was basted on top of the net. Cotton thread was used to embroider the design through both net and lawn. The needlewoman—perhaps young Miss Chauncey, a daughter of the merchant—cut meticulously around the first two floral sprigs, leaving the lawn visible only in a 1/4-inch wide strip above the scalloped edge of the collar. These were also freed from their paper pattern. The next four sprigs were embroidered but the mull is intact; two were released from the pattern, two are still basted.

The last few sprigs were not embroidered at all. It is, perhaps, comforting for today's needlewomen to know that even "back then," some projects were abandoned halfway through. We are fortunate that through whatever accidents of fate, this unfinished project survives to show us the processes used in the mid-19th century.

6930 Gift of Emeline A. Street

"White Embroidery comprises the art of working flowers, and other ornamental designs, on muslin, for dresses, or their trimmings; capes, collars, handkerchiefs, &c."

—"EMBROIDERY,"
Lady's Book, July 1, 1830

DAR MUSEUM

Chemisette

About 1840-1855

"And I shall look for thee in streets where dwell
The passengers by Broadway Lines alone!
And if my dreams be true, and thou, indeed,
Art only not more lovely than genteel—
Then, lady of the snow-white chemisette,
The heart which vent'rously cross'd o'er to thee
Upon, that bridge of sixpence, may remain—
And, with up-town devotedness and truth,
My love shall hover round thee!

–EXCERPT FROM "THE LADY IN THE CHEMISETTE WITH BLACK BUTTONS,"
The New Mirror, June 17, 1843

This lovely sheer lawn chemisette of the mid-19th century is simply constructed, with two pieces of lawn, joined only at the shoulder, tapering from a curved shoulder seam to about 7-inches wide at the waist. The lower edge of both front and back are drawstring casings for the woven cotton tape tie. A slit at the center back is fastened with a Dorset button.

The embroidery is an exquisite example of the delicate and intricate work capable of being done by machines, earlier than one would think possible. Sunflower-like flowers with padded satin-stitch petals are the dominant feature, accompanied by leaves made of various combinations of padded satin stitch and seed stitch, and grapelike clusters of tiny eyelets. A row of faggoting bordered by padded satin-stitch Vandykes (abstract pointed motifs, named after the style of lace in Van Dyck's 17th century portraits) meanders in a gentle wave to create a soft V-necked yoke effect, and is repeated at the neck.

Chemisettes developed out of the folded square or triangular kerchiefs Colonial women tucked into their low necklines. By the early 1800s, the chemisette, a simply constructed garment, often with a collar, was worn tucked into the bodices but also tied around the waist over the undergarments and underneath the dress. Most day dresses of the 1840s and 1850s when this chemisette originated, were fashioned with high necks, but a variant style had a wide open area at the neck to allow for the display of a pretty embroidered chemisette just like this one.

2001.65.3 Gift of Patricia Saunders

DAR MUSEUM

Nursing Gown
1840s

"She, who, for the pleasure derived from a party, can deprive her child of the food which nature had ordained for its use, is unworthy of the enduring title of mother."
–JOHN BRIGHT, *The Mother's Medical Guide*, 1844

This summer dress from the 1840s has more to tell us than its simple construction suggests. Under the edge of this fan-front panel is a more form-fitting bodice, with two slits for nursing a child. The fan-front style is found in innumerable photos of the 1840s and 1850s, and survives in many costume collections, yet is less common in fashion plates. Its adaptability to nursing and pregnancy may help explain its popularity: the style could also be made with drawstrings instead of fixed gathers at the waist, allowing adjustment for an expanding waistline. When not made for these events in women's lives, the fan-front would have been rather easier to fit than the usual bodices of this period, which were meant to fit smoothly over the corset.

It is worth noting that the waistline of this dress shows that its wearer had returned to her pre-pregnancy shape, yet is still nursing her child. Infant formula was unknown, and paid wet-nurses were uncommon. Moreover, doctors and parenting "experts" insisted it was a mother's sacred duty to nurse her child. Most children were weaned between the age of 1 and 2 years—but not in the summer, when children were more susceptible to diseases from contaminated water or unrefrigerated milk.

The fabric of this dress is white cotton with a tiny (1/8-inch) woven check, the bodice lined with plain white cotton muslin. The fan-front is gathered at the waist with 13 rows of shirring into a pointed waistline, which accentuated the narrow waist. Waistline, neckline and armscyes are all piped, typical for this period. The sleeve caps, wrists and fan-front are trimmed with 3/8-inch wide machine-made lace edging. The 131-inch circumference skirt is gauged into a 22-1/2-inch waist. The dress fastens in front with hooks and eyes. The wearer of this dress was petite, about 5 feet tall, and would have been considered tiny in her lifetime as well.

98.77 *Friends of the Museum Purchase*

DAR MUSEUM

Embroidered Corset

1830s

"If for ladies, they are made of sattine [sateen], or best French jean…[if of an inferior quality, they are made of white, brown, grey, or nankeen jean…] and lined with calico between the doubles. There are two gores on each side for the bosom, and two larger ones on each side below, for the hips.…It is as well to observe that unless particularly feeble, or otherwise an invalid, it is most desirable to wear as few bones as possible; and that for healthy persons, the two back bones, with the steel in front, are quite sufficient."

–THE WORKWOMAN'S GUIDE, 1838

The corset has had bad press since the flapper generation revolutionized fashion in the 1920s. But for most women of the 19th century, a corset was merely a critical undergarment, like a bra. Even without a bust in need of support, every woman required a corset to give her a smooth, conventional shape on which to fit her clothes. Dresses did not just hang on the body, but were fitted to the corseted form. Most corsets, like this one, were not the instruments of torture we think they were, and most women wore them sensibly, not excessively tight—except perhaps for that special occasion when a girl was willing to suffer for fashion—like wearing painfully high heels today!

This corset of the 1830s shows the curvaceous shape of that decade. With two bust gores on each side, it lifts the bust and supports it with cotton cording at the waist level. At center front, a casing held a brass busk, which curved to follow the female form, rather than trying to force it into an unnatural shape. Feminine tummy and hips were nothing to be ashamed of: the hip gores (two in front, two in back) allowed for some flesh, and the busk curved out over the tummy. The only bones in the corset are at either side of the center back opening, one bone each side, to make the corset hold its shape and not ride up on the body. There are 12 brass grommets on each side, slightly offset to facilitate the spiral style of lacing: one long cord was laced spirally, rather than criss-crossed as would be the style on later corsets.

The corset is made of a sturdy light-brown cotton twill called "jean"—the same fabric which, when dyed blue, gives us "blue jeans". It is lined in a slightly coarser, white jean. Each piece and its lining are sewn as one, edge to edge, to its neighboring piece, so that there are no seam allowances to annoy the wearer. (Corsets were worn over the chemise, but the bulk of seam allowances would have been uncomfortable.) Cotton cording helps give shape and support throughout the garment: two rows at the center of each gore and shoulder strap; 12 tiny rows at the top and bottom of the busk casing, with one long row on each side of the busk; a row beside each row of eyelets; and in front at the waist level, in a curvilinear herringbone-like pattern. This pattern is repeated in the back not just at waist level, but from shoulders to waist.

The only decorative elements are the delicate embroidered meandering vines in a pale tan cotton thread. Two vines wend their way on each gore and each shoulder strap, one on each side of the cording. Beside the vines, which resemble featherstitching, are tiny embroidered circles, which are not French

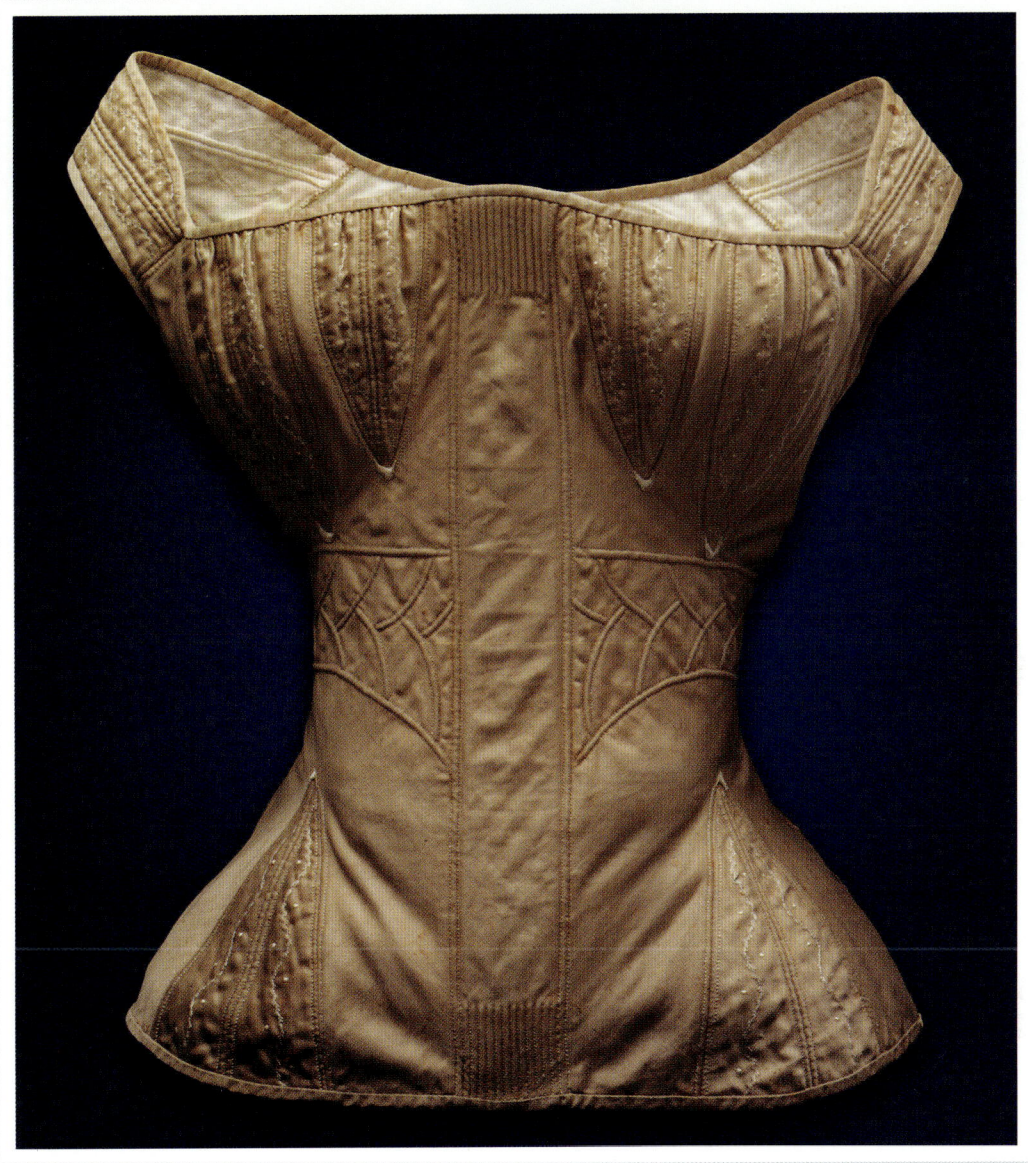

knots, but little "dots" or granitos made with just a few satin stitches. The embroidery and the cording form a restrained decorative element to this demure undergarment.

Margaret Johnson Seeber of Montgomery County, New York, owned this particular corset. As she was born about 1812, this may have been her wedding corset. Although we do not know the year of her wedding precisely, wedding corsets often had some demure decoration, and were saved in future years. Margaret may also have made it herself: professional corsetmakers were plentiful, but a style like this was not difficult to make at home. Godey's Ladies Book published a corset pattern as late as 1857. This one's waist measures 22-inches when closed—but engravings and paintings of the period confirm that, as Godey's sternly reminded its readers, "It must be remembered that stays ought not to meet when they are laced on." Margaret's waist was probably a healthy 24- to 26-inches.

48.49.1 Gift of Mrs. Alfred N. Abrams

"It was at length settled by Miss Martin's testimony, that the back parlor curtains were worsted damask instead of silk: that Mrs. Jorden always wore a cap at breakfast, and never came to dinner in her morning dress."

–"SCANDAL AND DRESS-MAKING," *Home Journal*, May 25, 1850

Blue and Brown
DRESSING GOWN AND WHITE TIERED PETTICOAT

1850s

The comfortably middle class lady of the mid-1800s spent her mornings in an outfit like this: a fitted dressing gown with a skirt that opened over an elaborately decorated petticoat skirt, embroidered en tablier (apron style), in a triangular panel at the front, the only place where it would be seen. In this outfit, topped by a frilly cap, she was fit to preside over her breakfast table, peruse her mail and go over her household accounts, and supervise servants, before dressing fully for her afternoon activities outside the house.

Brown and blue were a popular color combination in the 1850s. Ombré (shaded) silk and variations of weave and texture from matte to satin, add interest to the large-scale blue and black silk check of the dressing gown. Three decorative "buttons" on the bodice front are made of black silk, pleated around a blue pompon, with three dangling tassels (two are missing from the top button); the pockets on the skirt have matching button and tassels. The bodice fastens with 15 hooks and eyes from neck to waist, and is lined in white cotton. While the dressing gown was considered a form of undress, that is, an informal at-home garment, and its wearer might not be as tightly corseted as later in the day, it is by no means loose, with darts and bones in the bodice front to provide shaping and structure.

The dome-shaped skirt is knife-pleated into a 1-inch waistband in brown taffeta, which is also used in ruched trim throughout the gown. The ruching is designed to give an illusion of a small waist by curving down from the armscye and narrowing towards the waist, and then widening from 5-inches at the waist to 12-1/2-inches at the hem.

Additional ruching trims the hem, the pockets and the wide pagoda sleeves so popular in the 1850s. The sleeves and center front of the skirt are faced with brown taffeta near the edges, and lined in brown glazed cotton where it was unlikely to be seen. The neckline, back bodice seams, and even the seams between the panels of the skirt, are piped with brown taffeta; great care was taken to match the plaid of the fabric at these seams. Although the sewing machine was coming into use at the time this gown was made, this ensemble is entirely hand-sewn.

The cotton lawn petticoat alternates rows of pintucks (11, 10, 11, and 13 from top to bottom) with expanses of white-on-white embroidery and openwork in large-scale, machine-embroidered, scalloped designs, increasing from three to four to six, from top to bottom. The embroidered rows are integral to the skirt, not decorative insertions or ruffles. A final row of the same embroidery finishes the hem, both inside the front panel and all around the skirt. Three pintucks are positioned above the embroidery outside the front panel. The skirt is made in four panels with a 147-inch circumference gathered into a 27-inch self-waistband 1-3/4-inches wide; it opens at center back with a hemmed slit in the back panel and probably once had a hook-and-eye closure, now lost.

2005.53 (petticoat), 2006.20 (dressing gown)
Friends of the Museum Purchase

Anna Holyoke's WEDDING DRESS

1861

When this sumptuous but simple wedding gown arrived at the museum, neither the donors nor the curators at first realized that more than the bodice survived: the skirt had been removed from the waistband and carefully folded into what the donor explained was "an extra scrap." Unfolding the "scrap," we soon saw we had the complete skirt—still intact except for the waistband—and there beside it was the waistband, giving us the original dimension. Following the folds still visible at the top of the skirt, we were able to reassemble the skirt and recreate the wedding dress.

Many Victorian-era wedding gowns are low-necked evening dresses, which may seem odd until we realize that many weddings took place at home, and wedding dresses were often worn again by the young bride at formal dinners or dances in subsequent months. This sumptuous and simple white satin dress would have been an evening or ball gown for Anna Holyoke Cutts of Vermont, who wore it at her 1861 wedding. The enormous skirt, reflecting the peak of the crinoline style, is composed of six 29-inch-wide panels of Chinese silk sewn selvedge to selvedge and gathered in deep, double-stacked pleats onto a 26-1/2-inch waistband. Chinese characters in black ink are found in one selvedge, confirming the silk's origin. The hem of the skirt is faced for 6-inches above the hem with white cotton plain-weave facing, and is bound in a cream silk ribbon about 3/4-inch wide, of which only 3/16-inch appears on the face of the skirt.

The modestly low neckline of the bodice and pointed waistline in both front and back are piped, and its short flared sleeves are trimmed in silk tulle. Because of the deterioration of the tulle, it is difficult to discern what form this trim took: perhaps a sequence of puffs, or more likely (given its overall flatness) knife or box pleats. On the inside of the sleeve edges is a lightweight ivory silk box-pleated ruffle, about 1-inch wide, with pinked scalloped edges.

Two darts on either side of the center front seam provide shaping for a fairly generous bustline, and these darts, as well as all seams, are boned. White cotton twill lining is used throughout the bodice. Although buttons or hooks and eyes were in common use in day dresses of this time, evening gowns typically were laced; this bodice laces at the center back, with 16 pairs of eyelets. And while the sewing machine was readily available by 1861, all the seams in this bodice and skirt are hand sewn.

Anna's ivory silk tulle veil also survives, too fragile even to unfold, but able to be recreated for exhibition. It was a 49-inch square, edged all around with two rows of 1/4-inch wide tricot-edged ivory satin ribbon. Extra lengths of the silk used in Anna's dress were used to make part of her daughter Mary Cutts Howard's wedding dress in 1889, which the DAR Museum also owns.

96.10.1 Gift of Knute Malmborg

DAR MUSEUM

"A man ought to choose his wife, as Mrs. Primrose did her wedding-gown, for qualities that "wear well."

–"AUNT SUE'S SCRAP-BAG,"
Merry's Museum, Parley's Magazine, Woodworth's Cabinet, and the Schoolfellow, July 1860

DAR MUSEUM

Dressing Sacque
AND BUSTLE PETTICOAT

1880s

"Dressing jackets are made straight in front and semi-fitting at the back, the sleeves are rather loose and the neck is finished off with a very deep collar."
—"LADIES' DEPARTMENT. FASHION CHAT," *Saturday Evening Post*, May 6, 1882

Instead of a dressing gown, a young lady might wear a short dressing sacque (loose jacket) in the privacy of her room, over the petticoats that would later be covered by her dress. Here, a machine-made creamy lace jacket is cut in five pieces in the back, but merely shaped in front with side front seams. The center front opening hides five mother-of-pearl buttons and buttonholes under a ruffle of lace. The two-piece, set-in sleeves are very fitted, curving over the elbow and cut to slightly below 3/4-length.

The petticoat shown with this jacket is from the 1880s, and the cascades of ruffles in back would have helped give bulk to the bustle skirts worn over it. The front three-quarters of the skirt are shaped with darts to fit snugly over the hips. Featherstitching covers the seam joining the fitted skirt to the trimmed area below it. The rest of the skirt front is trimmed vertically with a series of four 1/2-inch pleats alternating with lace insertions appliquéd onto the petticoat. Near the bottom hem, the pleats release to create a full ruffle, trimmed with narrow net lace, which matches the appliquéd insertion lace.

The same lace trims the five ruffles at the back, which graduate in height from 4-1/2- to 6-inches. The skirt is on a drawstring, which, when gathered, creates the fullness of the ruffles. Under each ruffle is a second layer of gathered gauze, adding still more volume. A second drawstring is found inside the skirt at hip level, extending only across the ruffles, controlling their fullness.

92.90.9 Gift of Jane Ames, Barbara McAleer, and Virginia. Knull
2006.41.1 Friends of the Museum Purchase

DAR MUSEUM

Pictured left to right: Mary Emma Funk's Wedding Dress; Sarah Radcliffe's Wedding Dress; and Jean Mackay's Wedding Dress

"The bride's dress is marked by simplicity. But few jewels or ornaments should be worn, and those should be the gift of the bridegroom or parents. A veil and garland are the distinguishing features of the dress."

–MANNERS, CULTURE, AND DRESS OF THE BEST AMERICAN SOCIETY,
Richard A. Wells, 1891

DAR MUSEUM

Mary Emma Funk's WEDDING DRESS

1885

Rich, creamy satin is the most striking feature of this simple wedding dress worn in 1885 Philadelphia by Mary Emma Funk. The fashionably long bodice, or basque, extends just over the hips at the sides, and continues in front to a slenderizing V at center front, closing with 14 pearl shank buttons. The bodice, like most bodices of the mid- to late 19th century, was carefully shaped with four darts to fit snugly over the corseted body. A properly high neckline is finished with a narrow band collar, and long fitted sleeves are finished with the only embellishment of the dress, embroidered net lace cuffs at the wrist.

At the height of the bustle era, this skirt's fullness was very simply formed by draping the satin into a bubble-skirt effect, tucking the fabric underneath and anchoring it to a brown cotton skirt lining. The lower skirt is a series of box pleats from front to sides. The back of the skirt is cartridge-pleated into the waistband and falls into the modest train. The train is semi-detached in the last 12-inches of the skirt, allowing Mary Emma to walk in the otherwise rather narrow dress. Both bodice and skirt are fully lined in brown cotton twill coutil; the skirt has a 6-inch self-facing and a 2-inch lace-trimmed, knife-pleated, buckram "dust ruffle" under the hem of the train where it touches the floor.

While shown with a modern tulle veil draped in a fashionable manner for 1885, Mary Emma might also have worn a lace veil. Wax orange blossoms, an indispensable part of the bridal costume, were undoubtedly part of her headdress, and may also have been pinned to her dress. Dress, shoes and stockings accompany the dress, along with the dresses, shoes and stockings of her daughter and granddaughter, and her granddaughter's veil. The other dresses are featured elsewhere in this book.

96.92.1 Gift of Mr. James W. Christie, III, Mr. Stuart R. Christie, and Mr. John M. Christie

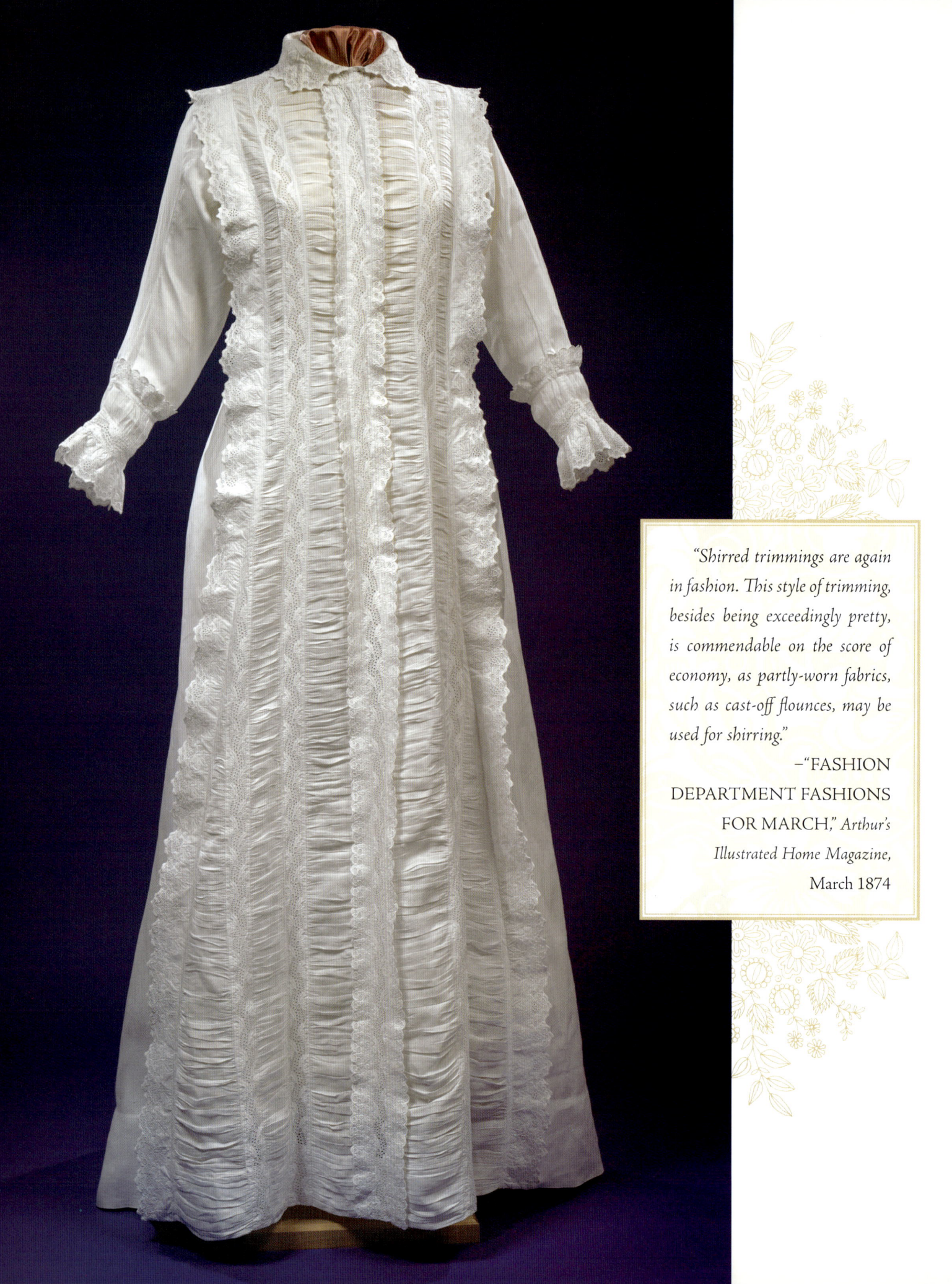

"Shirred trimmings are again in fashion. This style of trimming, besides being exceedingly pretty, is commendable on the score of economy, as partly-worn fabrics, such as cast-off flounces, may be used for shirring."

–"FASHION DEPARTMENT FASHIONS FOR MARCH," *Arthur's Illustrated Home Magazine*, March 1874

DAR MUSEUM

Young Lady's SHIRRED DRESSING GOWN

1870-80

This feminine dressing gown was worn by Annie Maria Robinson while attending college. Surely studying in one's room became a pleasant activity while wearing such a delectable garment!

The crisp white cotton gown is elaborately trimmed down the front panel with a symmetrical arrangement of bands of shirring and whitework embroidery insertions and edgings. The whitework consists of two different edgings of 1- and 2-inches wide, and a 1-1/4-inch wide insertion, all variations on the same pattern. The center band (a row of insertion framed within rows of the narrower edging) hides 3/8-inch buttons and buttonholes under a placket. A panel of shirred cotton, an insertion and a narrower band of shirring, flank the center panel on each side, ending with a ruffle of the wider edging. The ruffle has a scalloped edge with a grapelike cluster of eyelets and satin-stitched leaves, with needle-lace-filled eyelets paralleling the scalloped edge. This ruffle continues over the shoulders to define a deep, slightly pointed yoke with mitered corners in back. The yoke is filled with alternating vertical rows of shirring and insertions. A small fold-over collar is made of the wider edging. Long sleeves end in cuffs, which repeat (in simplified form) the trim on the gown's front: a band of the narrower edging, a 1-3/8-inch band of shirring, a row of insertion and finally a ruffle of the wider ruffle embroidery.

99.39.2 Gift of Ann Robinson King and Mrs. Samuel Fletcher King, Jr.

DAR MUSEUM

Alma Brooks's WEDDING DRESS

1892

This elegant dress of creamy silk, while perfectly appropriate for a wedding, would also adapt for use as a best evening dress afterwards, as was common even late in the 19th century. This was not only a matter of frugality; it was practiced even in well-to-do circles. Weddings were usually intimate family affairs, and by wearing the wedding dress to social functions afterwards, members of the bride's wide social circle had the opportunity to feel a part of the happy occasion. Alma Brooks wore this at her 1892 wedding to John Wason in Woodford County, Kentucky. It was worn by another family member, Margaret Wason Garett, in 1906 at her wedding to Dr. Ralph Tate in the same church.

The figured design on the silk is of abstract, large-scale but delicate feathery motifs. The bodice front is fairly simple, with an applied panel of the same figured silk. This panel has seven rows of cording gathered slightly to form shirring, and narrowing towards the pointed waist. The low, evening-style neckline is filled in with net appliqué lace, which continues into a high collar. The tape appliqué forms a symmetrical design of rosettes within a large medallion frame. The same lace falls below the neckline as a ruffle, the tape creating sprays of leaves, loops at the edges and a series of laurel wreaths. The ruffle falls below a strip of creamy satin with three rows of gathering stitches creating a slight ruching. A matching satin bow is applied over the ruffle at the center front of the neckline.

From the front to the back of the bodice, the figured silk gathers and drapes like a wide cummerbund. Four spiraling self-rosettes punctuate these gathers at center back. The sleeves have the moderate fullness of the early 1890s, which in a few years will evolve into the huge leg-of-mutton style. At the elbow is a gathered band of barely off-white silk chiffon, less creamy than the rest of the dress, with a double pouf on the outside of the sleeve. Below the chiffon is an appliqué lace ruffle layered over a ruffle of creamy mousseline de soie (sheer soft silk, thinner than chiffon) with a slight crimp in the weave edged in a 1/2-inch wide slightly ruched self-binding.

The skirt is virtually undecorated, fitting close over the hips. It has two pleated satin inserts in the front (matching the bodice bow), that measure 21-inches from knee level to hem. Each insert has six deep knife pleats facing center; the upper edges of the inserts are slightly diagonal, edging up 1-1/2-inches from inner to outer corner. The skirt is unlined, but has a 3-1/2-inch deep piped, self-reinforced hem and, inside the hem, a 3-3/4-inch deep dust ruffle of lace-edged, knife-pleated buckram. The dress came with a separate cream taffeta petticoat with a knife-pleated flounce.

2005.34.1 Gift of Margaret Garrett Shropshire

"At parties given to a newly married couple, the bridesmaids and groomsmen are always invited, and the whole party are expected to wear the same dresses as at the wedding."

–FLORENCE HARTLEY,
Ladies' Book of Etiquette and Manual of Politeness, 1875

Redwork Embroidered COMBING JACKET

1885-1900

Those legendary "hundred strokes" of the hairbrush that every woman was supposed to give her hair each day were often done while wearing a combing jacket. The jacket would catch the strands that fell out, which could be saved to make hair "rats" to plump out the pompadour hairstyles of the turn of the 20th century. This jacket was made from a diaper-weave linen towel, and embroidered in redwork so popular at the time. The comb and brush motif might have been copied from a ladies' fashion or needlework magazine. The towel was simply cut partway up the center to create an opening, with a circle cut out in the middle for the neck; twill tape binds the edges and is used for neck ties. We do not know who "PGS" was, but she undoubtedly looked lovely at her dressing table.

75.90 DAR Museum

"How different is the description of the marriage of the Earl of Derby. Perfectly modest, inasmuch as no mention is made of a trousseau, let alone stockings, combing jackets, and corset covers."

–"GODEY'S ARM-CHAIR, EXTREME SNOBBERY," *Godey's Lady's Book and Magazine*, October 1870

Aesthetic Style
WISTERIA TEA GOWN

About 1900

Today, dealers or collectors may call almost any vintage day dress of the turn of the century a "tea gown" as long as it is made in a particularly feminine style that evokes a tea or garden party. But the term has a much more specific meaning: it was used to describe an informal, flowing gown popular for at-home wear beginning in about 1880.

This exquisite example of a true tea gown is as loose as a wrapper, unlike many tea gowns on which flowing front panels concealed inner structures that were not much comfier than wearing a corset. It is made of mauve taffeta and constructed quite simply, with front panels, two-piece coat sleeves with self-cuffs, and a four-piece back with curved princess seams extending from the armscye down to the hem.

The entire gown, including the sleeves, collar and front panel, is lined in a soft silk of vivid lavender, quilted in a horizontal lozenge (diamond) pattern. An inch-wide strip of folded lavender silk with fringed ends is sewn into the lining at the back to create a tie at the waist. The small fold-over collar shows some signs of alteration, as some of the embroidery has been cut off on the standing band underneath it.

The front panel of delicate lilac-colored silk (not quite chiffon but even lighter than China silk) is attached underneath the taffeta on the left, and fastens with flat self-covered buttons at the right, in a concealed button placket. Despite being buttoned all the way down at approximately 5-inch intervals, the lilac silk is sewn to the taffeta for 12-inches above the

> "Tea-gowns, despite the name, are not worn at teas, nor is any semi-loose garment suitable in which to appear in public. They originated at English country-houses, and were found convenient to slip on after returning from a ride or drive before dressing for dinner....In America they are worn occasionally by ladies who receive every week in the season, or at very small luncheons, and are supposed to indicate great informality."
>
> —ETIQUETTE FOR ALL OCCASIONS, Mrs. Burton Kingsland, 1901

hem. The front panel has honeycomb smocking at the waist, which repeats in a chevron pattern at the neck. Above the smocked neckline, the modest V is filled in with silk tulle, which continues into a 2-inch standing collar, boned with wavy wires at intervals to keep its shape; three snaps fasten the collar at center back.

The most striking feature of the tea gown is, of course, the abundance of wisteria clusters, which spill down the front of the dress on either side of its opening and around the hem. The clusters graduate in size from shoulder to hem, and are embroidered in variegated silk. The overall color of the clusters alternates between pale and richer purples. More wisteria decorates the cuffs and collar, and tiny clusters of blooms adorn the soft silk center panel, almost hidden in its folds until the wearer walked. The back also has two wisteria blooms trailing down each shoulder.

While many tea gowns were simply informal afternoon gowns that allowed women to wear something slightly less constricting than what was required outside the home, some may have been enjoyed during pregnancy. The lack of structure in this one, and its apparent excess of fabric in the front, is suggestive of this use.

2007.10 Gift of Louisa Eifrig Pineault

Creamy Satin WEDDING GOWN

1904

The sumptuous creamy satin of this gown is deftly manipulated to create numerous textured embellishments, giving the dress a luxurious effect while observing the prevailing rule of tasteful simplicity in wedding dress design. Helen Hodgson Baily wore this dress when she was married to Robert Alexander Blackford in St. John's Episcopal Cathedral in Norristown, Pennsylvania in September 1904.

The dress consists of three pieces: bodice, skirt and a boned belt. The bodice is deeply V-necked, front and back; the Vs are filled in with shirred satin panels and the rows of shirring are about 1/2-inch apart. The standing satin collar has three rows of shirring at the center and is edged with a 1/4-inch wide pleated ruffle of fine silk net. It is detached except at center front and is fashioned with wiring at the top and bottom edges, together with vertical bones placed every 2-inches to keep it stiff and erect. The remainder of the bodice is draped in wide, soft pleats from the shoulders to create the effect of a wrapped, surplice bodice. The pleat closest to the center on the right is edged with net lace embroidered

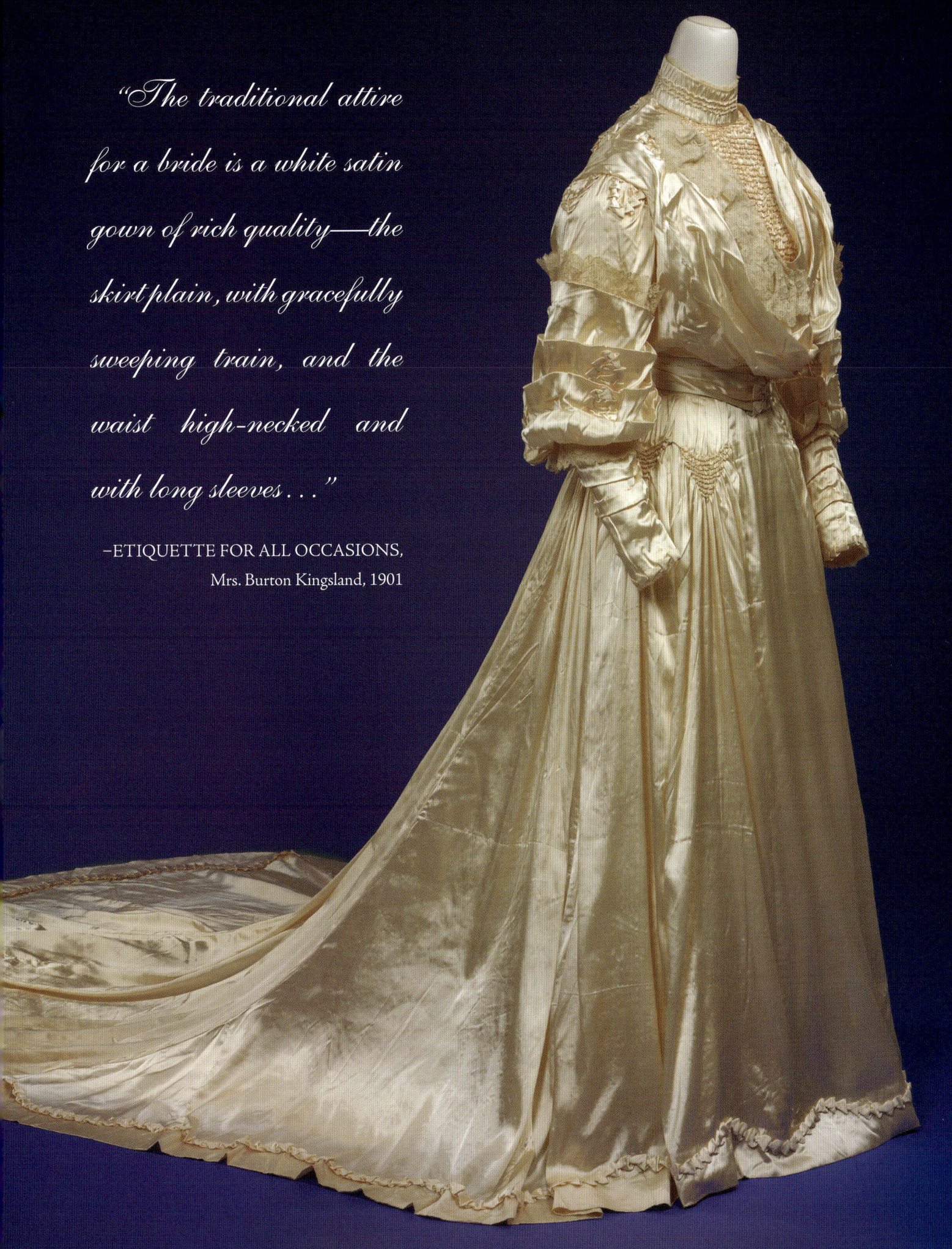

"The traditional attire for a bride is a white satin gown of rich quality—the skirt plain, with gracefully sweeping train, and the waist high-necked and with long sleeves…"

—ETIQUETTE FOR ALL OCCASIONS,
Mrs. Burton Kingsland, 1901

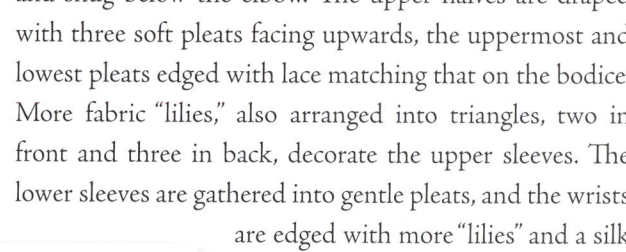

with large daisy-like flowers and leaves. Each shoulder is decorated with two triangular areas in which matching satin pieces have been manipulated into a series of trumpet or lily-like shapes emerging from one another.

The sleeves are fashionably full at the shoulder and snug below the elbow. The upper halves are draped with three soft pleats facing upwards, the uppermost and lowest pleats edged with lace matching that on the bodice. More fabric "lilies," also arranged into triangles, two in front and three in back, decorate the upper sleeves. The lower sleeves are gathered into gentle pleats, and the wrists are edged with more "lilies" and a silk net ruffle. The sleeves close with three hooks and eyes.

The skirt is less ornate with repeats of the same decorative motifs. At hip level, around each side of the skirt, three triangular areas of shirring, nine rows in each, contain the fullness pleated into the waistband, releasing it to create the stately train. Above the hem of the skirt and train, another chain of "lily" folds meanders in a gentle wave. The boned belt, nearly hidden by the bodice drapery (the close-up photo shows the drapery pinned up), has triangular areas of shirring at the back, and four self-ribbon bows fastening it at the front.

All the accessories for the wedding were donated with the dress—the veil and orange blossoms decorating it; the stockings; and the satin shoes—the right one specially fitted with a white kid-covered metal brace to attach to a leg brace for the bride, who had survived polio.

2006.29.1 *Gift of Beverly H. Blackford*

DAR MUSEUM

Gauze Over Silk
EDWARDIAN GOWN

1905

Cream silk gauze is lined with creamy silk and embellished with shirring and lace in this feminine dress of about 1905.

The bodice offers most of the decoration, with an unusual center-front, hook-and-eye closure on both the gauze and lining, concealed by a vertical ruffle of gauze. (At the turn of the century, complicated off-center openings were more common.) The gauze at center front falls gently in the fashionable pouter pigeon drape, which forms part of the fashionable S-curve silhouette of the day. This fullness is gathered into two groupings of five rows of shirred tucks, one below shoulder level, and the other just above the bustline. A flange of net appliqué lace flanks these panels. A dart on each side is neatly hidden between the lace and the gauze in the lower part of the bodice. The lace is repeated in the high collar, which is edged with a 1/2-inch wide ruffle of ivory silk chiffon. The collar is detached from the bodice on the left side from center front to center back, has one piece of boning on the left edge, and fastens with hooks at the

> "The dress of the future will follow the conditions of the future women. It is prettier and daintier to-day than it ever was and as long as women continue pretty and dainty there is little fear that the graces of costume will vanish."
>
> –"THE FUTURE OF DRESS," *Harper's Bazaar*, June 1904

back. Additional hooks along the bottom edge on the detached side fasten to the dress along the left neck edge to prevent gaps.

The bodice back echoes the center-front panel gathers and lace flanges, but in simpler format. A gauze waistband gathered into vertical rows of shirring at front and back, forms a moderate point at center front; this would have accentuated both the curve of the hips and the narrow waist. The bodice is lined in a lightweight, crisp, cream silk taffeta with satin binding on the neckline and waist.

The elbow-length sleeves, so typical of the middle of the first decade of the 20th century, derive most of their fashionable fullness from the effect created by the gathers in the gauze. They, too, are lined in lightweight silk. Four vertical bands of gauze puffing are bordered and created by a series of five rows of gathering stitches. The undersides of the sleeves are not gathered. There are eight rows of shirring at the cuff, beneath which falls a lace ruffle matching the lace flange and collar.

The skirt consists of three panels of gauze fitted over the hips at front and sides and in two deep pleats in back on either side of center. It is fashioned over a cream silk satin underskirt and fastens in back with hooks and eyes.

Strips of gauze ruching run horizontally above the hem for 14-inches, looping upward at intervals in the front and sides of the skirt to meet vertical ruched strips. Seven lace medallions are spaced around the skirt above the horizontal ruched strips, four of them framed by the vertical ruching. The medallions consist of bobbin lace looped into three ovals. The large center oval frames a flower made from two layers of chemical lace petals in imitation of point de venise, with bobbin lace stem and leaves, and a three-dimensional, machine-made, domed button center.

Around the bottom of the skirt are five ruffles of the same net as the skirt, each edged with 1/2-inch wide machine-made lace. Of these ruffles, the top two are appliquéd onto the skirt, and the bottom three are 1-inch wide self pleats.

The cream silk underskirt has five gored panels and a knife-pleated self-flounce at the hem, 7-inches deep. The ruffle has two rows of hand-stitched gathers 3/4-inch below the top, machine-stitched to the underskirt to create a header ruffle; the flounce is trimmed with the same lace edging as the ruffles near the hem of the gauze overskirt. Inside the lining skirt is a 7-inch deep dust ruffle of white muslin with a 2-inch flounce trimmed with the same lace edging as the other hem ruffles. The muslin is also used to make a small bustle inside the center back of the underskirt: although the bustle era had passed, little pads or ruffles at lower-back level were often used to create the curvaceous silhouette of the period.

96.50.3 Gift of Judd and Dianne Fitze

"The picture of a group of girlish students clad in their white or light-tinted gala robes... appeals strongly to the poetic sense, for in it seems incarnated one's ideal of feminine purity and loveliness. Only simple, youthful modes are deemed correct for either school or college graduates."

–THE DELINEATOR,
May 1894

DAR MUSEUM

Lingerie Style GRADUATION DRESS

1907

This lovely lingerie dress was worn by the donor's mother, Laura Jones Simon, at her graduation from high school in Morris, Illinois in 1907. White dresses were associated both with youth and innocence, and with life's milestones—baptism and marriage both required white—and were adopted for graduation from schools and colleges in the 19th century. Cotton wash dresses were popular for summer wear in the early 20th century; with their infinite variety of tucks and insertions they were perfectly suited to these occasions. Laura went on to complete a degree at Illinois Women's College, and we also have her 1909 graduation dress, another lingerie dress with embroidery and lace in an updated style.

The decoration of this dress depends on alternating plain cotton with two types of machine-made lace insertions in chevrons. Rows of machine-made net lace with a small floral sprig motif, sewn edge to edge, form the yoke of the bodice, which zigzags above the first chevrons. Below the yoke, lace (with a nearly identical but larger-scale floral motif matching that of the yoke) makes the first set of chevrons. The second type of lace is almost a large-scale faggoting with a machine-made imitation bobbin lace grid at each edge and large open areas in the middle. This openwork lace alternates with the net lace throughout the dress. Beneath the first chevrons on the bodice, pintucks release above another chevron-shaped repeat of lace insertion, cotton and lace. The remainder of the bodice is cotton draped in a modified pouter pigeon pouf that was on its way out of fashion by 1907.

The waistband is made of two rows of openwork lace with net between them, the upper row of openwork extending up near the side seams. The above-elbow-length puffed sleeves have the same chevron-shaped insertion. The puffs are gathered into cuffs of openwork lace and net, the openwork pointing up at the outer part of the sleeve to make the cuff larger. Each cuff ends in a ruffle of edging lace on which the floral motif echoes, but differs slightly from, the insertion laces.

Beginning above knee level are two wide bands with double chevrons repeating around the skirt, consisting of two rows of insertion with a narrow band of cotton between them. These bands are sandwiched between bands with one row of openwork between two rows of net lace. At the hem, two pintucks and a 1/2-inch tuck are placed beneath the final row of net lace.

The dress opens at the back to below the waist with 24 hooks and crochet-loop eyes; the armscyes are bound, and the rest of the seams are French.

99.8.5 Gift of Mary Lou Niemants

DAR MUSEUM

Henrietta Malone's DAINTY NIGHTGOWN

1910

"Every woman loves and always will love, a betwitching bit of lingerie and many dainty trifles that are truly feminine."
—"SOME PRETTY LINGERIE TRIFLES," *Harper's Bazaar*, February 1910

This dainty nightgown belonged to Henrietta Steele Malone of Mobile, Alabama. A yoke of Swiss embroidered cotton with floral sprays and eyelets descends in two tabs at the front, which are outlined with 1/2-inch wide lace insertion. The yoke is entirely finished with a shallow satin-stitched scalloped edge at top and bottom. Above the yoke are buttonhole openings for a shell-pink ribbon insertion, which acts as a drawstring. The neckline is finished with a lace ruffle, which matches the lace outlining the embroidered tabs of the yoke.

The slightly puffed, three-quarter-length sleeves are cut in one piece, pintucked vertically around the elbow, and set in with a ladder-stitch seam. The sleeves are finished with embroidered cuffs matching the yoke, including an embroidered tab on each sleeve outlined with the same insertion. This lace also forms an edging for the cuffs.

The body of the nightgown is made from two pieces French seamed at the sides. The back has twelve 1/2-inch released pintucks; the center front has 44.

2006.34 Gift of Ellan W. Thorson

DAR MUSEUM

Sarah Radcliffe's WEDDING DRESS

1914

"And with the gown, lace and seed-pearl embroidery, lovely enough to dream about, but all of it subordinated to the beautiful, stately lines of the dress itself.…for the wedding-dress the law of dignity, beauty and simplicity should be absolute, inviolable."

—"NOW COMES THE BRIDE," *The Delineator*, June 1911

Sarah Cunningham Radcliffe wore this intricately draped dress at her Philadelphia wedding in 1914. The slender lines of the early 1910s, and love of asymmetry and contrasting textures in fabrics combine here to form an elegant dress at the height of the prevailing mode. The complex construction makes it almost impossible to describe intelligibly in detail, leaving the modern observer wondering how the fashion writers of the time ever managed to convey these styles to their readers!

The dress is made of luscious, creamy satin with sleeves of silk tulle edged in satin bias binding. The binding, being bulkier than the net, causes the sleeve layers to undulate in graceful three-dimensional waves. Under the tulle, a fall of elegant lace completes the sleeve. Satin bias tubes, echoing the sleeve binding, drape over the bodice and enhance a panel over one hip. A boned 4-inch wide band of cream silk taffeta provides a structural underbodice, which, along with a silk net bodice, is attached to a China silk underskirt. The satin and tulle are draped over this underpinning along with a beautifully arranged satin surplice bodice; the neckline is filled in with a net tucker. Originally, lace to match that on the sleeves was sewn atop this net, but it was removed to make the Juliet cap for Sarah's daughter, whose 1942 wedding outfit is pictured elsewhere in this book.

The skirt is draped up at the left knee-level in front with a tulle and satin rosette; at back, the skirt drapes into a short asymmetrical fish-tail train. A separate, rectangular train, 84-inches long, falls from the waist, widening from 11- to 20-inches; its underside is edged with a 3-inch wide knife-pleated tulle ruffle. The veil and vintage orange blossom headpiece in the photo are not original to Sarah's outfit, but recapture the style from her wedding photo as accurately as possible.

96.92.7 Gift of Mr. James W. Christie, III; Mr. Stuart R. Christie; Mr. John M. Christie.

DAR MUSEUM

Pictured left to right: Mary Emma Funk's Wedding Dress; Sarah Radcliffe's Wedding Dress; and Jean Mackay's Wedding Dress

"Whatever fits men and women for good citizenship fits them for marriage—the requisites for either begin a sound body and a sound and enlightened mind, and a good conscience."

—"SOME THOUGHTS ABOUT MARRIAGE AND DIVORCE," *Herald of Gospel Liberty*, September 1914

Jean MacKay's WEDDING DRESS

1942 with lace from 1914

Jean Radcliffe MacKay, the daughter of the 1914 bride and granddaughter of the 1885 bride in this book, was married in this dress and veil in early February of 1942. Although America had entered World War II just two months earlier, Jean would have ordered her dress before Pearl Harbor. Thus, she would not have been affected by imminent rationing as would later wartime brides, and her full-length dress, with its magnificent train, violated no restrictions.

The slightly off-white satin rayon dress—rayon being considered as elegant as silk—is, like her mother and grandmother's, perfectly in keeping with contemporary wedding dress style. It has a sweetheart neckline and long sleeves with medieval points over the hand; the sleeves fasten at the wrist with three snaps. The neckline and armscyes are piped, as is the slightly dropped, self-piped waistline on which the effect is heightened by another row of self-piping at hip level. The fabric between waistline and hipline is cut separately from the skirt. The skirt gathers release into the generously full skirt and enormous train.

The white silk tulle veil extends to nearly the end of the train, as wedding dress etiquette demanded. The Juliet cap of lace, another fashionable style for the 1940s, was made from lace taken off of Jean's mother's 1914 wedding gown, and formed her "something old." In addition to the dress and veil, Jean's wedding shoes—ivory satin open-toed sandals with a slight platform—are also part of the Museum's collection. We are extraordinarily fortunate to have three generations of brides' outfits in an organization that treasures family history.

96.92.11 Gift of Mr. James W. Christie, III; Mr. Stuart R. Christie; Mr. John M. Christie.

DAR MUSEUM

Ivory Satin WEDDING WAISTCOAT

1830

"It was the custom of the higher order of Teutones, a people who inhabited the northern part of Greece, to drink mead or metheglin, a beverage made with honey, for thirty days after every wedding. From this custom comes the expression 'to spend the honey-moon.'"

–"VARIETIES," *The New-York Mirror*, January 2, 1830

Soft ivory silk satin is embellished with creamy satin-stitch floral embroidery to make an elegant and dressy wedding waistcoat worn by Thomas Fielder Bowie of Prince George's County, Maryland, who married Catherine Harrison Waring in 1830. Thomas and Catherine were the great-grandparents of the donor. White waistcoats were often a groom's nod towards wedding attire, worn with everyday trousers and coat appropriate to the time of day; the waistcoat, special to the occasion, was often saved.

This waistcoat is distinctly different from earlier styles, as it reflects not only developments in men's fashions, but also new tailoring techniques: the simple flat construction of 18th century waistcoats has given way to a multi-layered garment, which attempts to create the popular curvilinear silhouette of its day. The collarless and standing collar styles have likewise given way to a preference for lapels, providing more surfaces for embroidery.

Here, roses and other flowers meander up the lapels, while a rose in a medallion on each side of the center front opening is the focus of the embroidery on the body of the waistcoat. Below the medallions, thorny branches extend to the bottom of the waistcoat and along its lower edge. More floral embroidery decorates the tiny pocket flaps on either side; an additional unembroidered breast pocket flap is found on the left side. The pocket flaps and lapels and front opening are edged with an extremely thin ivory silk cording. The waistcoat closes with five silk thread buttons and silk-thread-bound buttonholes.

Shaping is provided in several ways. There is a dart near each side seam, but it is the inner layers that provide the most three-dimensionality. Several layers of cotton batting (at least three that can be determined), in graduated sizes atop each other basted to an interlining of muslin, provide subtly rounded shaping. This padding begins just above the embroidered pockets and extends up to within a few inches of the shoulders.

The front opening is faced with the same satin as the waistcoat, a continuation of the satin lapels, except for a 2-inch high patch of ivory figured silk near the hem on both sides. The remainder of the waistcoat is lined in white cotton; the same cotton forms the outer layer of the waistcoat's back. Glazed white cotton straps sewn at the side seams and extending to the back, secure a brass buckle used for fitting the waistcoat more snugly to the body.

62.57 Gift of Ruth Bowie Houghton

Embroidered Cotton SLEEVED WAISTCOAT

About 1725-1740

> *"Farewell to my rags!—for at one time my coat,*
> *And waistcoat, and breeches no buttons had got!*
> *So I dress'd on a morning with needle and thread,*
> *And doff'd them with scissors when ready for bed!"*
>
> —EXCERPT, "FAIRWELL TO DRUNKENNESS," *The Religious Intelligencer*, January 10, 1835

Waistcoats of the first half of the 18th century often had sleeves, as this one does, with the lower sleeves decorated to match the body of the garment, as they would peek out from the sleeves of a gentleman's coat. This waistcoat is cotton, although its somewhat irregular threads create a slightly striated effect in the weave and suggest linen. Such a summer-weight garment was popular in the southern American colonies, for obvious reasons. The waistcoat is lined throughout in linen, and the embroidery was stitched through both the outer fabric and a linen backing, making three layers in the front panels.

The center front opening has no closures. Lining the opening and the bottom of the waistcoat are wide bands of golden yellow silk embroidery of elaborate abstracted decorative motifs in a rather rococo style. Six-inch wide pocket flaps, embroidered in a coordinating style, partially cover one repeat. Lively sprigs of stylized carnations bound with bow-knotted ribbons and sprays of indeterminate flowers and leaves grace the open areas beyond these edges. As men's styles of the early 18th century featured generously cut coats and waistcoats, the lower part of this waistcoat flares and has side and back vents. Cheery floral vines climb up the edges of the back vent. The sleeves are cut generously enough to contain the fullness of a gentleman's shirt sleeves, but not excessively so, as they must fit under the sleeves and wide cuffs of the (outer) coat. The sleeves are embroidered to match the torso below the slits at the outer sides of the wrist.

99.16.2 Gift of Mrs. Charles R. Angel

"It is now become difficult to distinguish on a Sunday, a journeyman barber from a younger gentleman, an heir to a barony, an apprentice from his master, or a maid from her mistress: a footman dressed up in a cast-off laced waistcoat and a flourishing wig, shall frequently pass for my lord; and a poor fellow, who all the week long shall be treated with the greatest contempt, in his plain working dress, as a mean insignificant wretch, on a Sunday, dressed up in his best, shall be esteemed a companion even for Mr. Churchwarden himself."

—"ON THE PRESENT SENTIMENTS WITH RESPECT TO DRESS,"
The Royal American Magazine, August 1774

DAR MUSEUM

Rococo Swags
CUTAWAY WAISTCOAT

1770s

Since the owner of this waistcoat was killed at the Battle of Lexington in 1775, we have a good cutoff date for it. Major General Joseph Warren was better known for his medical prowess than his fashions: he inoculated thousands of Boston residents for smallpox during an epidemic of 1763-4, thereby saving many lives and making his own reputation, after which he became one of Boston's leading physicians. He was an associate of the Boston patriots, including John Hancock and the Sons of Liberty, and was the man who sent Paul Revere and others on their midnight rides to alert the countryside to the British troops' approach. A silk waistcoat does not speak particularly of these political involvements, but certainly he would have looked quite the beau wearing this elegant waistcoat with its delicate sprigs and swags of silk embroidery on ivory satin on some special social occasion.

Tiny rosebuds alternate with miniscule white floral sprigs on the front of this waistcoat; silver and silk ivory leaves, rosebuds and leafy sprigs outline the neckline, center front and lower edge. Elegant swags of ivory leaves, roses and pendant bunches of ivory flowers adorn the mock pocket flaps, and are repeated below the pockets. The buttons are outlined in silver thread and feature a tiny rosebud in the center of each.

The front edges of the waistcoat are faced in ivory silk; the remainder of the front pieces is lined in linen. The back pieces and narrow side pieces are ivory wool, also lined in linen. Waistcoats like this were embroidered professionally in Europe on a narrow width of silk, and were pieced by a tailor to fit the American customer. Often the silk was not wide enough to make front pieces wide enough to reach to the side seams. Many waistcoats, therefore, like this one, have extra side panels under the arm with scraps of the fashion fabric pieced near the bottom where it might have been seen. The front panels were also evidently too small at the neck: two triangular pieces of satin were added to the back of the neckline to make the waistcoat large enough over the shoulders.

56.24 Gift of Miss Caroline Sherman, Miss Dorothea Sherman and Gertrude S. Littlepage

DAR MUSEUM

Inaugural Ball
TAFFETA WAISTCOAT

1789

"About noon, the illustrious Washington appeared, and as he passed under the first triumphal arch, the acclamations of an immense crowd of spectators rent the air, and the laurel crown at that instant, descended on his venerable head."

—"AN ACCOUNT OF THE PREPARATIONS OF GRAYS FERRY…",
The Columbian Magazine, May 1789

The restrained elegance of this waistcoat would have qualified it to grace the most elite events of its day, and in fact, it reputedly was worn by Colonel Thomas West Peyton of Virginia to George Washington's 1789 Inaugural Ball in New York. If this history is correct, it was a conservative style, for the new style in waistcoats was shorter. Still, older gentlemen often stayed faithful to familiar, less cutting-edge styles.

The ivory silk front is embroidered with small floral sprigs and sprays; the buttons echo these motifs with one small sprig each. The bottom of the "skirt" is cut away on either side of center front for 6-inches below the last button, typical of waistcoats from about 1770 through the mid-1880s. The front is lined with linen; the back is made entirely of linen. A gusset of a different linen at center back tapers from a point 4-1/2-inches below the neck to 3-1/2-inches wide at the hip, and probably was an alteration to allow for extra girth. Fine waistcoats like these would have been kept and worn for several years. Side pieces of linen are original to the garment.

The entire waistcoat is lined in linen, the seams felled.

54.118 Gift of Victoria Thornburg Vickers

DAR MUSEUM

Thomas Rumrill's WEDDING WAISTCOAT

1793

"A Wedding's a wedding the universe over,
From Perkin to London, from Turkey to Dover;
Married folk are the same, wherever they're born,
From Cape of Good Hope till you double Cape Horn."
—EXCERPT FROM "COURT OF APOLLO," *Weekly Museum*, August 22, 1795

Thomas Rumrill of Roxbury, Massachusetts would have looked elegant and fashionable wearing this creamy satin double-breasted waistcoat at his 1793 wedding to Abigail Richardson. The off-white was less related to the wedding than to current neoclassical trends in men and women's fashions; ivory and cream waistcoats were the most fashionable for dressy occasions. This one is truly double-breasted, with buttonholes, buttons and embroidery placed to allow buttoning in either direction. Like most waistcoats, the back is a plain, rather coarse linen—why use good fabric where it would not be seen? The entire waistcoat is lined in a finer linen. These waistcoats are not cut close to the body, but as with many waistcoats, this one has two sets of linen woven-tape ties at the center back, which would have allowed for some fitting to the body.

The embroidery on the waistcoat consists of branches of brown, ivory, green and silver thread, branches with silver spangles (flat sequins), and stylized wheat sheaves in brown and rose. The collar and revers (lapel) repeat the foliage sprays that adorn the center front and the mock pocket welts, and the motifs are connected by embroidered light and dark blue serpentine vines. All edges of the collar, revers, center front and waistline are outlined in a wavy light brown satin-stitch embroidered design. The buttons are embroidered in eight-pointed star designs composed of ivory chain-stitched crosses over rose-pink chain-stitched crosses.

The wheat sheaves were not only a popular emblem during the Federal period; they symbolized fertility, and may have been chosen consciously for a wedding. Thomas and Abigail had seven children; Abigail died shortly after her daughter Metilda was born in 1801.

1430 Gift of Miss Ellen W. Rumrill

DAR MUSEUM

Young Boy's SATIN WAISTCOAT

About 1770-1785

"I saw a spruce young fellow, with an elegant silk waistcoat, satin breeches, superfine coat, silk stockings, set knee buckles, shoe-buckles a-la-mode de Londres, a hat cocked with ineffable grace, and a fine bamboo cane."
—"HARD TIMES," *The Columbia Magazine*, September 1786

This young boy's waistcoat shows a transitional period in men's styles. The waistlines of men's waistcoats rose at the same time that waistlines of women's dresses rose during the 1780s and 1790s. A seam runs horizontally across this waistcoat just above the pockets, indicating an alteration: either the waistcoat was cut down from a man's, or the boy's garment was shortened to keep up with fashion. The cutaway style of the lower part of the waistcoat is a holdover from waistcoats of the 1760s and 1770s, while the shorter length, standing collar and neoclassical-style embroidery represent the newer fashions of the 1780s and 1790s.

The waistcoat is oyster-colored silk satin, and was probably always somewhat darker than the usual cream or ivory waistcoat color for this period. The front opening is embroidered with blue and light tan chain-stitched silk in abstract serpentine vines, with blue, brown and green leaf sprigs. The pocket flaps are embroidered with flowers, medallions and floral swags, repeated below the pockets. Floral and feather sprays are scattered across the body of the waistcoat. As commonly found on American waistcoats of the 18th century, this one is lined in linen with two pairs of linen tie tapes at the back, to adjust the fit.

50.12 *Gift of Genevieve Hendricks*

Cherry Red
WINTER WAISTCOAT

About 1825-1830

"Having set my plate of soup too near the edge of the table, in bowing to Miss Dinah who politely complimented the pattern of my waistcoat, I tumbled the whole scalding contents into my lap."
—"ADVENTURE OF A BASHFUL MAN," *The New Jersey Monthly Magazine*, April 1, 1825

The cheerful cherry red silk satin and colorful embroidery of Jonathan Collins's waistcoat reminds us that men's clothing had not completely lost its decorative qualities in the second quarter of the 19th century. Two stylistic details help us pin down a date range of about 1825 to 1830: the straight waistline seen on waistcoats of the first quarter of the century had given way to slightly rounded or pointed ones, just barely visible here; and the standing collar disappeared after 1830. The waistcoat shows evidence of being altered from an earlier style, so the fabric may date earlier.

The waistcoat is embroidered in wool chain stitch with floral sprigs about 3- inches apart, and floral vine intertwined with ivory ribbon-like vine with bowknots along the center front, bottom hem and collar. Eight buttons embroidered in four-petaled flowers march down the center front. The collar is constructed of three pieces, and lined with ivory silk twill.

The back panel is off-white heavily napped wool flannel for warmth. Side panels have been added as an alteration, the upper parts of flannel, the lower 3-inches of satin. Both side and front panels are lined in the same ivory silk twill as the collar, and the side panels are interlined with white linen.

54.187 Gift of Miss Florence C. Hays

DAR MUSEUM

Figured Silk ALTERED WAISTCOAT

1790s

"For this well-timed bounty our traveler presented her with two of the four brass buttons which remained on his waistcoat."

—"SELECTIONS," *The Monthly Magazine, and American Review*, June 1799

Rising waistlines and slimming silhouettes were the trend in women's fashion in the 1790s, and men's clothes echoed this: coats became less full and waistcoats shortened to nearly waistline level. This waistcoat of the 1790s reflects these changes with its straight edge and shorter length. Its colorful chain-stitch embroidery on off-white silk also harkens back to earlier styles like those worn by Joseph Warren and Thomas Peyton and featured elsewhere in this book. In fact, it may have been altered from an earlier waistcoat. Silk cut from the bottom cutaway "skirt" may have been repurposed to form the collar.

The silk here is a figured silk; a woven design with vertical stripes between rows of floral sprigs. The front and lower edges are embellished with sprays of pink roses, green sheaves of grass and blue flowers, connected by a delicate serpentine line. The 2-1/2-inch standing collar has embroidered figured silk only in the front 4-1/4-inches. The pattern of the floral sprays and the position of the serpentine waves on the collar pieces show that the left collar piece may have been cut from the right front of the waistcoat, and the right collar piece from the left front.

The false pocket flaps have been incorrectly attached. Waistcoats such as these arrived in America pre-embroidered by professional embroiderers in France and England, ready to be cut and fit to a customer by an American tailor. The tailor in this case mismatched the pocket flaps, as the stripes do not align: they were reversed, the narrow stripe and the wider stripe with the leafy design in the middle should have matched on both sides. Eight buttonholes on the left and small holes on the right side of the opening, indicate where buttons once fastened the waistcoat.

The waistcoat front and collar are lined in linen, and the back is a single layer of unbleached, lesser-quality linen. Even the well-to-do saw no point in wasting good fabric where it wasn't needed nor would it have been seen.

56.19 Gift of Martha Waugh Smith Boyle

The page of history informs us, that the progress of any nation in morals, civilization, and refinement, is in proportion to the elevated or degraded position in which woman is placed in society; and the same instructive volume will enable us to perceive, that the fanciful creations of the needle, have exerted a marked influence over the pursuits and destinies of man.

–THE LADIES' WORK-TABLE BOOK, 1845

DAR MUSEUM

EMBROIDERIES

The embroidery designs shown are a sampling of the many patterns featured on the antique garments. These may be enlarged for hand embroidery or are available for machine embroidery (all formats) on CD-ROM from Martha Pullen Company.

Empire Waist Infant Gown

Charlotte Knox's Baptismal Dress

Back-Fastening Child's Frock

Back-Fastening Child's Frock

Federal Era "Seamless" Baby Gown

Federal Era "Seamless" Baby Gown

Pleated Yoke with Smocked Bodice

Ayrshire Work Toddler Dress

Ayrshire Work Toddler Dress

Cornucopia and Curlicue Ayrshire Dress

Cornucopia and Curlicue Ayrshire Dress

Cornucopia and Curlicue Ayrshire Dress

Cornucopia and Curlicue
Ayrshire Dress

Cornucopia and Curlicue
Ayrshire Dress

Cornucopia and Curlicue
Ayrshire Dress

Cornucopia and Curlicue
Ayrshire Dress

Cornucopia and Curlicue
Ayrshire Dress

Appliquéd Floral
Embroidered Dress

Appliquéd Floral
Embroidered Dress

Appliquéd Floral
Embroidered Dress

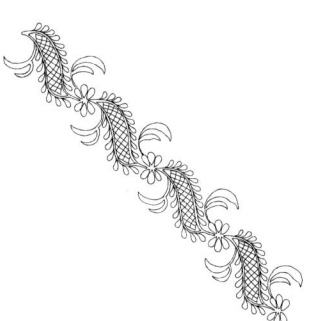
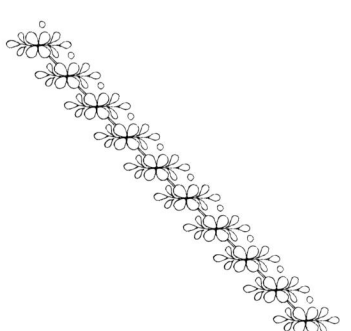

Raglan Sleeve
Muslin Dress

Raglan Sleeve
Muslin Dress

Fifty-One Pleats
Baby Dress

Mary Ann Nickerson's
Christening Dress

Gathered Bodice
Summer Dress

Thomas Rumrill's
Wedding Waistcoat

Young Boy's
Satin Waistcoat

Young Boy's
Satin Waistcoat

Cherry Red
Winter Waistcoat

Inaugural Ball
Taffeta Waistcoat

Inaugural Ball
Taffeta Waistcoat

Cherry Red
Winter Waistcoat

Cherry Red Waistcoat

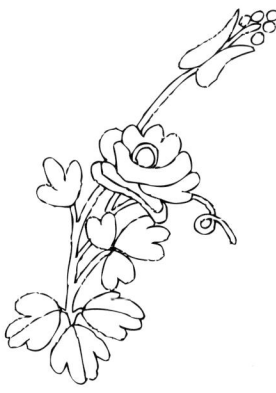
Figured Silk
Altered Waistcoat

Figured Silk
Altered Waistcoat

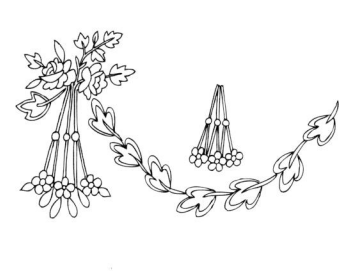
Rococo Swags
Cutaway Waistcoat

Rococo Swags
Cutaway Waistcoat

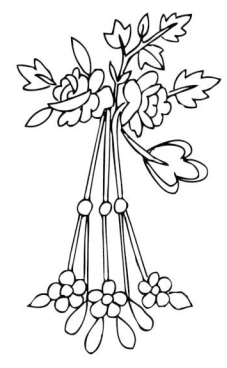
Rococo Swags
Cutaway Waistcoat

Embroidered Cotton
Sleeved Waistcoat

Embroidered Cotton
Sleeved Waistcoat

Embroidered Cotton
Sleeved Waistcoat

Embroidered Cotton
Sleeved Waistcoat

Embroidered Cotton
Sleeved Waistcoat

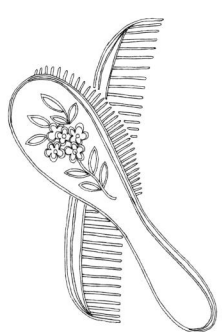
Redwork Embroidered
Combing Jacket

Henrietta Malone's Dainty Nightgown	Center Panel Embroidery Mull Dress	Center Panel Embroidery Mull Dress	Embroidered Transparent Muslin Gown
Embroidered Transparent Muslin Gown	Chemisette	Chemisette	Chemisette
Ivory Satin Wedding Waistcoat	Ivory Satin Wedding Waistcoat	Ivory Satin Wedding Waistcoat	Ivory Satin Wedding Waistcoat
Ivory Satin Wedding Waistcoat	Ivory Satin Wedding Waistcoat	Aesthetic Style Wisteria Tea Gown	Aesthetic Style Wisteria Tea Gown